Science and Faith

Science and Faith

Proceedings from
the Twenty-First Annual Convention of
The Fellowship of Catholic Scholars

September,1998
Denver, Colorado

Gerard V. Bradley, J.D. and Don De Marco
Editors

ST. AUGUSTINE'S PRESS
South Bend, Indiana
2001

Manufactured in the United States of America.

2 3 4 5 6   07 06 05 04 03 02 01

Library of Congress Cataloging in Publication Data
De Marco, Donald
    Science and faith : proceedings from teh Twenty-First
    Concention of the Fellowship of Catholic Scholars, 1998
    / edited by Gerard V. Bradley and Don de Marco.
      p. cm.
    Includes bibliographical references.
    ISBN 1-890318-80-9 (alk. paper)
    1. Religion and science – Congresses. 2. Catholic Church
    – Doctrines – Congresses. I. Bradley, Gerard V., 1954–
    II. De Marco, Donald. III. Title.
BX1795.S35 F45 2000
261.5'5'08822 – dc21   00-008720

∞ *The paper used in this publication meets the minimum requirements of
the American National Standard for Information Sciences – Permanence of
Paper for Printed Materials, ANSI Z39.48-1984.*

Contents

SCIENCE AND FAITH: INTRODUCTION
Don DeMarco...vii

1. ALPHA AND OMEGA: RECONCILING SCIENCE AND
   FAITH
Charles J. Chaput, O.F.M. Cap. 1

2. FAITH AND THE STRUCTURE OF LIFE
Michael J. Behe...13

3. FAITH AND THE STRUCTURE OF THE COSMOS
Stephen M. Barr..35

4. FAITH AND BIOLOGICAL REDUCTIONISM: DARWIN
   AS A RELIGIOUS REFORMER
F. F. Centore 50

5. FAITH AND PROCREATION: THE FIGHT FOR THE
   FUTURE
Germain Kopaczynski, OFM Conv...............................68

6. FAITH AND THE THERAPEUTIC CULTURE
William Kilpatrick..100

7. SOCIALIZATION: A THEOLOGICAL PERSPECTIVE
Cynthia Toolin...118

8. SCIENCE, FAITH, AND ATHEISM
Don DeMarco...137

9. AN UNSCIENTIFIC POSTSCRIPT ON CATHOLICISM IN
   AN AGE OF SCIENCE
Archbishop George Pell 147

Fellowship of Catholic Scholars 165

SCIENCE AND FAITH:
Introduction

Don DeMarco

A few years ago, while on a lecture tour in Australia, I had the pleasure, while in Canberra, of being a guest at the home of Sir Peter Lawler, former Ambassador to the Vatican from Ireland. His position of diplomatic privilege had allowed him, upon occasion, to be on personal terms with His Holiness, John Paul II. One statement in particular that the Holy Father conveyed to him stood out in Sir Peter's mind. "The Pope said to me with considerable earnestness," my genial host informed me, "Don't make an idol of science."

John Paul has a way of being able to communicate to the whole world, even when speaking privately to but a single person. His warning has a firm foundation. Society makes an idol of science whenever it teaches that science is not only our *highest* source of truth, but also it *only* source. "We now live," as playwright Arthur Miller has expressed it, "in an air-conditioned nightmare." "Why," the existentialist Albert Camus asked, "has the Enlightenment led to the Blackout?" We are strong in the face of things, neglectful of persons; technologically sophisticated, morally callow.

In June of 1980, in his address at UNESCO, the Pope stated that "Men and women of science will truly aid humanity only if they preserve the sense of the transcendence of the human person over the world, and of God over the human person." We find in this brief sentence not only an affirmation of the Holy Father's respect for science and regard for humanity, but his recognition that the former can serve the latter only if it does not absorb it into itself. Science should <u>serve</u> humanity, not dominate it.

The Catholic Church is not against science. What it is against is turning science into an idol, and consequently using science as a way of oppressing humanity. It is against the secular use of science to oppose the unique and transcendent value of the human person.

A synonym for the Age of Science is the Age of Anxiety. The world has experienced, under the weight of science, the diminishment of man. In filling his head with facts, man has bled his life of wisdom. Edna St. Vincent Millay made note of this phenomenon several decades ago when she made the following comment:

> Upon this gifted age, in its dark hour,
> Rains from the sky a meteoric shower
> Of facts . . . they lie unquestioned, uncombined.
> Wisdom enough to leech us of our ill
> Is daily spun, but there exists no loom
> To weave it into fabric

The Pope understands the importance of this "loom" which integrates knowledge in the context of wisdom. He does not use the word "loom." Rather, he refers to it as the "heart of the Church." He begins his statement on higher education, "*Ex Corde Ecclesiae*," by reminding us that, historically, it was from the "heart of the Church" that Catholic education was born.

The mind separates through analysis, the heart integrates through comprehension. When science becomes an idol, the world becomes fractionalized. Science and faith, ind and body, facts and values, reason and emotion become alienated from each other. Cartesian dualism becomes triumphant and the "heart of the Church" lies dormant.

Neurological researcher Antonio Damasio, for one, believes, he has found scientific evidence that refutes this dichotomy. In his intriguing study, *Descartes' Error: Emotion, Reason and the Brain*, Damasio states that "Emotion may well be the support system without which the edifice of reason cannot function properly and may even collapse."

Science does not validate its own initial assumptions. It does not explain, scientifically, how the cosmos got to be intelligible in the first place. It does not explain the natural affinity that exists between microcosm man and macrocosm world. Yet it cannot proceed without an abiding faith that the world in intelligible and orderly, and that man is a knower of reality and not merely a thinker of thoughts.

Albert Einstein once remarked in words that have an unmistakable Augustinian ring, that "There are only two ways to live your life. One is as though nothing is a miracle. The other is as though everything is a miracle." Science begins only after it has unscientifically accepted the miracle of the intelligible cosmos and its inherent implication of a transcendent force or Designer that lies beyond the stars. For this reason, Arthur Koestler has described scientists as Peeping Toms at the keyhole of eternity, an image which has an irresistible affinity with that of Catholic philosophers as Peeping Thomists at the window of the Eternal Law.

The "Queenly Sciences," Philosophy and Theology, as well as the "Soft Sciences," such as Psychology and Sociology, together with the "Hard Sciences," such as Physics, Biology, and Chemistry, all bear testimony to the existence of a reality that transcends their narrow limits as particular sciences. Our conference brings together several notable scholars from a variety of sciences who not only know much abut their respective disciplines, but something of the larger picture that they imply.

We are about to leave the present millennium that began in the Dark Ages to enter the new millennium that lies before us. Let us make this temporal journey with the abiding hope that the spiritual values which the idolization of science has suppressed for too long will re-emerge, healthy and vigorous, forming a strong alliance with Science so that a new synthesis between Science and Faith will nourish both our minds and hearts, and with them, our appetites for both knowledge and wisdom.

Dr. Donald DeMarco
Program Chair

ALPHA AND OMEGA: RECONCILING SCIENCE AND FAITH

Charles J. Chaput, O.F.M. Cap.

The Voice From the Whirlwind

First of all, I want to thank you for having me as your guest tonight. I've admired the Fellowship of Catholic Scholars for many years. I know many of you personally and consider you friends, so this isn't a routine official welcome. I want you to know you're most welcome here in Denver, and you have my best wishes and prayers for a very fruitful conference.

So far today we've heard three outstanding presentations on cosmology and biology. Now, to quote the great English theologian John Cleese, it's time for something completely different. By training, I'm neither a scholar nor a scientist. But I am a pastor. As a pastor, I deal with the practical effects of this theme – faith and science – every day. My job is to preach and teach the truth about the human person. The United States in the late 1990s is the premier scientific power in the world. American culture is dominated by technology – the child of science – in a way which is unparalleled in history. And Americans are the greatest pragmatist and toolmakers in human experience. That's part of our national personality. We're inquisitive. We're innovative. We like results, and science is a profoundly useful tool. So to the degree that faith and science are perceived to differ about the nature of the human person, every pastor faces a challenge in his ministry.

I believe the Holy Father is right when he says that no fundamental conflict can exist between science and religious faith, whatever the appearance to the contrary. Truth can't contradict itself, and both science and faith are means to discovering truth about creation. But their estrangement is often still very real, and that's what I'd like to reflect on tonight. Why is there a "disconnect" between them, and how do we fix it?

In trying to answer that, I'm going to observe the good scientific principle of parsimony and keep my thoughts simple and short. In fact, I have only three basic observations, and then perhaps we can open the floor to questions and general discussion, because I came here as much to learn as to teach. But I want to approach my first point in a roundabout way. We heard earlier this afternoon about the cosmological order and biological reductionism. I'd like to talk instead about the theology of B movies.

How many of you remember what a B movie is? How many of us here tonight were born in the 1940s or earlier? A good number. Those of us who are in the general vicinity of 50 have something uniquely in common: We're the first generation of the atomic era. Our memories are conditioned by that. Some of you will recall the air-raid drills of the 1950s. Remember how we would climb under our desks at school, hoping they'd protect us from a nuclear blast?

And some of you may also remember the films. I don't mean the big-screen, Cadillac releases like *Ben Hur*. I mean the low-budget, black and white titles like *The Blob*, which starred a giant, man-eating amoeba; Them, which starred giant, man-eating ants; and *The Attack of the 50 Foot Woman*, which starred a giant, taxi-crushing Amazon. I've always believed that painting, music, literature, architecture – each of these is a window on the psychological and spiritual state of people. The popular media, like B movies, serve exactly the same purpose. They're clues to our hope and anxieties – crude one, it's true, but sometimes amazingly accurate. In most of the B movies of the 1950s, a scientific accident – usually involving radiation – triggers an out-of-control monster who's defeated only by luck, or by an even more ingenious scientific countermeasure. Each of these movies point to a deep popular ambivalence toward science. We desire the power science brings. But we also fear its consequences, because deep-down we instinctively realize that we lack the ability to control what we unleash. Like Pandora, we've opened a box filled with surprises – and not all of them are welcome. We've released a whirlwind of change that threatens to unhinge all our notion of coherence.

The main value today of most of these old B films is curing insomnia on late night cable TV. But I mention them because one of these films stands out as a very interesting anomaly. How many of you have seen *The Incredible Shrinking Man*? Does anyone remember the ending? It's pretty unusual.

Here's the plot: The hero is an average, innocent, middle-class fellow who, one day, get hit by a random burst of cosmic radiation. That's all the explanation we ever get. A few days later, he notices that his clothes are a bit loose. Gradually he discovers that he's actually shrinking. He goes to the doctor. The doctor does tests, gives him a shot and reassures him that science will find a cure. But it doesn't. He continues to shrink until he's the size of a mouse, and then an insect. At this point he has a fairly standard, B-movie, life-and-death struggle with a house spider – which now seems the size of an elephant, by his scale. He kills the spider, but the effort exhausts him. In the movie's final scene, he drags himself to a basement window and looks out – and then upward – through a forest of grass, to a night sky blazing with stars. And this is what he says:

> "I looked up, as if somehow I would grasp the heavens. The universe – worlds beyond number, God's silver tapestry – spread across the night. And in that moment, I knew the answer to the riddle of the infinite. I had thought in terms of man's own limited

dimension. I had presumed upon nature. That existence begins and ends – this is *man's* conception, not nature's. And I felt my body dwindling, melting, becoming nothing. My fears melted away, and in their place came acceptance. All this vast majesty of creation had to mean something – and then I meant something too; yes, smaller than the smallest, I mean something too. *To God, there is no zero . . .*"

Now, I certainly don't want to invest a low-budget science-fiction film with the moral gravity of the ages. Nor do I usually have the time to watch anything on TV, let alone *The Incredible Shrinking Man*. But the message of this strange little story is almost unique among its genre: Life has meaning, no matter how battered or small; God is good, and the universe reflects His design; and creation is infinitely more vast and mysterious than our ability to control or even understand it. It sounds familiar, doesn't it? Let me remind you where we've heard that message before: Job 38 and 40.

"Then the Lord answered Job out of the whirlwind. . . Where were you when I laid the foundation of the earth? . . . Have you commanded the morning since your days began, and caused the dawn to know its place? . . . Have *you* an arm like God, and can you thunder with a voice like his . . . ?"

And this is my first point. The appropriate posture of man and woman before God, and science before God's creation, is humility – the virtue which Bernard of Clairvaux called *verissima sui agnitio*, "the truest knowledge of oneself," and Newman described as the "reverential spirit of learners and disciples." Even for those who do not know God or do not believe in Him, the lesson is the same: Science uninformed by modesty in the face of its own limitations will end by dehumanizing the humanity it intends to serve.

Pride, including scientific pride, kills the human spirit. The evidence of this century is irrefutable. We are not gods. We will never by gods. And to be in right relationship with nature, *we must never seek to be gods*. It may not be intentional, but it's certainly very curious, that the shrinking man of our 1950s movie only discovers truth and peace as his former self literally melts away.

The Beginning of Wisdom

The first point leads to my second: Human happiness is not a function of worldly knowledge, including scientific knowledge. Knowledge sometimes creates as much misery as comfort. We all know hundreds of facts which really add nothing to our lives. Does it help you to know that the surface temperature of Venus will boil lead? Unless you're an exobiologist, probably not. No, happiness flows from meaning, the discernment of which requires wisdom.

Let me share with you another story. Most of us know Taylor Caldwell through her novel about St. Luke, *Dear and Glorious Physician*. But she wrote many other things and one of her lesser known but most intriguing novels is a book called – if I remember it correctly – *Dialogues with the Devil*. The structure of the book simple. It's an exchange of letters between two polite but estranged brothers – in this case, the archangels Lucifer and Michael – who argue over the policies of their Father, who is, of course, God.

In one of his letters, Lucifer describes a room in the afterlife reserved for scientists who have knowingly and willfully rejected God. It has no demons. No fire. No instruments of torture or discomfort of any kind. In fact, just the opposite. Every tool of scientific inquiry is immediately available. So is every reference book. So are unlimited data about anything which any scientist would ever hope to know. Only one thing is missing: *purpose*. In rejecting God, they've rejected the One Being who gives context and meaning to all knowledge; the Whole who completes all the fragments of information which science laboriously acquires and studies. That's their eternity. They know everything . . . and yet they also know it's empty without the one priceless piece they've thrown away forever.

That's an unflattering portrait of some scientists, I admit. My only defense in using it is that I'm sure the room set aside for bad archbishops is even worse. You get the idea, though: Human happiness may be enriched or advanced by scientific knowledge, but it's not finally *about* knowledge. It's about who we are, and why we're here. Science can't address that. Despite all its power, science has some very severe limits. Quantum physics can predict that certain particles will behave in a certain way with a superb degree of reliability . . . but it really has no idea *why* they behave that way. Science can't even attempt to answer the ethical questions it raises, because of the moral neutrality it enforces upon itself.

Ironically, it was the great scientist Pascal who observed the "the heart has its reasons which reason cannot know." Science is fundamentally – *by its nature* – inadequate to the hungers of the heart. Poetry and art and religious faith speak to those hungers, and those hungers are very real, no matter how many attempts are made to explain them away as biochemically based projections or neuroses. You see, we can live without a lot of data. But we can't live without a purpose. And science has no competence to provide one. That in itself is tremendously revealing of the kind of creatures God designed us to be.

I have one final, cautionary thought about science, and it has to do with its bloodline. "Science" is an interesting word. It traces itself back to the Latin verb *scire* (to know) and the Latin noun *scientia* (knowledge). Science, defined in popular terms. Is knowledge covering general truths or the operation of general laws – especially as obtained, tested and refined through the scientific method. What science has done in the 500 years since Francis Bacon lived and wrote, is to provide living proof for his claim that "knowledge is power." Bacon is the earliest salesman for today's "knowledge societies." Knowledge works. It's useful. American technology is a global witness to it. Scientific knowledge has brought us many tremendous benefits, from antibiotics to electric lights. But the spirit of utility at the heart of applied science is something with which *none of us* should feel entirely comfortable. Knowledge may be power, but it's not the same as moral character, joy, love, freedom or wisdom – the things that sustain the human heart. Today's science and technology, in fact, have an ambiguous family history. In *The Abolition of Man*, C.S. Lewis reminds us that, "The serious magical endeavor and the serious scientific endeavor are twins: One was sickly and died, the other strong and throve. But they were twins. They were born of the same impulse."

I'm not sure many scientists would welcome the idea that Great Grand Uncle Albert may have been a sorcerer. But Lewis, who was an impeccable scholar, makes a pretty strong case. "For the wise men of old," he says, "the cardinal problem had been how to conform the soul to reality, and the solution had been knowledge, self-discipline and virtue. For magic and applied science alike, the problem is *how to subdue reality to the wishes of men*: The solution is a technique; and both, in the practice of this technique, are ready to do things hitherto regarded as disgusting and impious." If this sounds alarmists, let's remember that eugenics; partial birth abortion; physician-assisted suicide; cloning; cross-species experiments; and genetic manipulation were all just crazy ideas for low budget, B-grade horror films when C.S. Lewis was writing 40 or 50 years ago. Now they're here. Now they're real.

When you go home tonight, or back to your hotel room, open your Bible to Psalm, 111, or to Sirach, chapter 1. They're very similar. Listen to these words of the psalmist, which I've taken at random from the test: "Great are the works of the Lord . . . full of honor and majesty is His work . . . *holy and terrible* is His name! . . . Blessed is the man who fears the Lords" because "*the fear of the Lord is the beginning of wisdom.*" And then listen to these verses from Sirach, 1:11 and 12: "The fear of the Lord is glory and exultation, and gladness and a crown of rejoicing. The fear of the Lord delights the heart, and gives gladness and joy and long life."

It is *natural* for the human heart of find joy in "the fear of the Lord." And by fear I mean the awe we instinctively feel in the presence of something great, mysterious and beautiful. The universe is more than dead matter and impersonal equations. Wisdom enables us to see this. And wisdom is what we lack when reason separates itself from faith. It's a kind of poverty, for too many scientists, that their vocabulary for understanding truth covers only one dialect.

I am the Alpha and Omega

If you have a spare summer day when you're visiting Denver sometime, here's a suggestion: Get up at 4 a.m. and drive west on Interstate 70 about an hour until you reach U.S. Route 6. Take 6 west to the top of Loveland Pass. Park you car, wait for the sunrise, and then hike north along the Continental Divide trail. Every great artist has a "signature," some habit of craft that's unique and which everybody immediately recognizes. For Van Gogh, it's probably his brush strokes in a painting like Starry Night. The high Rockies at sunrise – that's God's signature. Anyone who comes away from a moment like that without sensing that nature is somehow *sacramental*, something sacred which hints at Someone even greater than itself, just doesn't have a pulse.

I began my comments tonight by asking why the estrangement between science and faith still persists, and how we might fix it. I suspect that religious believers sometimes make matter worse by expecting too much from Scripture and tradition. To quote C.S. Lewis again:

> "Christians . . . have the bad habit of talking as if revelation existed to gratify curiosity by illuminating all creation so that it becomes self-explanatory and all questions are answered. But revelation appears to me to be purely practical, to be addressed to the particular animal, Fallen Man, for the relief of his urgent necessities – not to the spirit of inquiry in man for the gratification of his liberal curiosity. We know that God has visited and redeemed His people – and that tells

us just about as much about the general nature of creation, as a dose given to one sick hen on a big farm
tells *it* about the general character of farming in
England."

In his statements on Galileo, evolution, and in a hundred different other environments, Pope John Paul II has
recognized the legitimate autonomy science must exercise
in its pursuit of truths about creation, and as recently as his
Wednesday audience of Sept. 16, he stressed again that the
Church is the friend of any sincere and ethical human
research. This merely echoes what Vatican II taught so artic-
ulately in the *Pastoral Constitution on the Church in the
Modern World (Gaudiem et Spes)*:

> "[M]ethodical research in all branches of knowledge,
> provided it is carried out in a truly scientific manner
> and does not override moral laws, can never conflict
> with the faith, because the things of the world and the
> things of faith derive from the same God. The humble
> and persevering investigator of the secrets of nature is
> being led, as it were, by the hand of God in spite of
> himself, for it is God, the conserver of all things, who
> made them what they are"(36).

From the perspective of science, of course, the rational-
ist-material prejudices which scientists inherited from the
Enlightenment continue to drive many of them away from
the deeper truth found in religious faith. But as others at
this conference have already noted, times are changing as
the "argument from design" has gained new strength.
Anyone who hasn't seen the August 1998 issue of *Scientific
American* should pick up a copy and browse through the
article entitle "Beyond Physics: Renowned Scientists
Contemplate the Evidence of God." While the writer certainly doesn't take a Catholic approach to these issues, listen to the following quotations from the article:

> "There is a huge amount of date supporting the exis-
> tence of God," asserts George Ellis, a cosmologist at

the University of Cape Town and an active Quaker, "The science of the 20th century is showing us, if anything, what is unknowable using the scientific method – what is reserved for religious beliefs," [adds] Mitchell P. Marcus, chairman of computer science at the University of Pennsylvania. "In mathematics and information theory, we can now guarantee that there are truths out there that we cannot find . . .

"The inability of science to provide a basis for meaning, purpose, value and ethics is evidence of the necessity of religion," says Allan Sandage [one of the fathers of modern astronomy] – evidence strong enough to persuade him to give up his atheism late in life. [Meanwhile, George] Ellis, who similarly turned to religion only after he was well established in science, raises other mysteries that cannot be solved by logic alone: "The reasons for the existence of the universe, the existence of any physical laws at all and the nature of the physical laws that do hold – science takes all of these for granted, and so it cannot investigate them."

"Religion is very important for answering these questions," Allan Sandage concludes.

This brings me to my final point. The way science will regain its soul, the way science and faith will begin one day to work together to serve the truth and advance real human dignity, is through the witness of intelligent women and men of faith, like yourselves. The Fellowship of Catholic Scholars has come a long way in a short time. Believe me when I say that God is using all of you as missionaries to a new areopagus, where people have a desperate need for God but don't have the language to even ask for your help.

Your faith in Christ Crucified – as scholars and writers, teachers and scientists – is a very powerful form of evangelization. You preach the Christ who is Alpha and Omega, the beginning and end of all things; the One in whom the natural and the divine, the spiritual and the material, science and faith, are reconciled. I mentioned earlier that poetry, like art and religious faith, is one of those things that speaks to the hungers of the human heart. I'm not much good a reading poetry in public, but there's a poem by Ranier Marie Rilke – it's called "Evening" – which captures so beautifully some of the things we've been talking about tonight. I encourage you to read it and reflect on it. Listen just to the final verse:

To you is lest (unspeakably confused)
your life, gigantic, ripening, full of fears,
so it, now hemmed in, now grasping all,
is changed in you by turns to stone and stars.

This is the human predicament: part clay, part glory; a story told crudely in low budget films and elegantly in high poetry; studied and measured by science; redeemed by God's son . . . and lived by each of us. The reconciliation of faith and science, I suspect, takes place first in our own hearts. And it begins when we say "I believe" – and we mean it.

Thank you, and God bless you all.

Addendum

EVENING

Slowly now the evening changes his garments
held for him by a rim of ancient trees;
You gaze: and the landscape divides and leaves you,
one sinking and one rising toward the sky.

And you are left, to none belonging wholly,
not so dark as a silent house, quite
So surely pledged unto eternity
as that which grows to star and climbs the night.

To you is left (unspeakably confused)
your life, gigantic, ripening, full of fears,
so it, now hemmed in, now grasping all,
is changed in you by turns to stone and stars.

Rainer Maria Rilke

FAITH AND THE STRUCTURE OF LIFE

Michael J. Behe

Introduction

In the early nineteenth century a chemist named Friedrich Wöhler heated ammonium cyanate and was astonished to find that a substance called urea was formed. To most people today the result is about as interesting as reading a list of ingredients on the back of a can of processed food. Wöhler's work, however, had far-reaching scientific and philosophical consequences with which we continue to wrestle. Ammonium cyanate, it turns out, is an "inorganic" chemical – one that is not derived from living material. Urea, however, is a biological waste product. Wöhler's synthesis of urea from inorganic chemicals shattered the easy distinction between life and non-life and opened up for scientific study all biological phenomena. After more than a century and a half of investigation, scientists have explained much of life. We have cracked the genetic code, solved the mystery of heredity, discovered the structure of DNA. Life scientists engineer genes to cure diseases and produce more abundant crops. Stories appear almost weekly in major newspapers, detailing this or that astonishing advance in science's control over life.

Now, here is an interesting question: since Wöhler's work showed that the stuff of life is ordinary physical matter, and since studying the properties of matter is the job of science, why am I here today taking up your time? Why does this concern the Catholic Church? Why should the physical processes which govern the formation of life interest the Church any more than processes which form snowflakes or mountain ranges? Well, the obvious answer is that *we humans* are living things, too. Furthermore, we know though our faith, and through philosophical and theological reflection, that humans are not merely physical objects. Rather in us are somehow combined both physical and non-physical elements. Therefore, both science and religion have a legitimate interest in the question of how life works and how it got here. Pope John Paul II made this clear in his statement to the Pontifical Academy of Sciences last October.

> The church's magisterium is directly concerned with the question of evolution, for it involves the conception of man. . . . The human individual cannot be subordinated as a pure means or a pure instrument, either to the species or to society; he has value per se. He is a person.[1]

Nonetheless, in his statement the pope acknowledged that a theory of evolution is a legitimate scientific conclusion, noting that:

> the encyclical "Humani Generis" considered the doctrine of "evolutionism" a serious hypothesis, worthy of investigation and in-depth study equal to that of the opposing hypothesis.[2]

But the pope also realized that there is more to a theory of evolution than just a collection of facts:

> Rather than the theory of evolution, we should speak of several theories of evolution. On the one hand, this plurality has to do with the different explanations advanced for the mechanism of evolution, and on the other, with the various philosophies on which it is based. Hence the existence of materialist, reductionist and spiritualist interpretations.[3]

[1] Pope John Paul II, *L'Osservatore Romano* (Oct. 30, 1996).

[2] *Ibid.*

[3] *Ibid.*

Thus the pope divides a theory of evolution into two separate components: 1) the mechanism whereby life was first produced and then diversified; and 2) the philosophy that is attached to the mechanism by proponents of the theory. He clearly condemned materialistic interpretations of evolution.

> Theories of evolution which, in accordance with the philosophies inspiring them, consider the spirit as emerging from the forces of living matter or as a mere epiphenomenon of this matter, are incompatible with the truth about man.[4]

Charles Darwin's claim to fame, of course, is that he proposed a completely naturalistic mechanism whereby evolution might take place. Before Darwin's time the similarities between different species of living organisms had led several scientists to propose that living things are related by descent from a common ancestor, but no one could imagine what might cause organisms to change. In retrospect, Darwin's elegant theory seemed to be simplicity itself. He observed that there is variation in all species. He reasoned that since limited food supplies could not support all organisms that are born, the ones whose chance variation gave them an advantage in the struggle for life would tend to survive and reproduce, outcompeting the less favored ones. If the variation were inherited, then the characteristics of the species would change over time. Over great periods, great changes might occur. Darwin had hit upon a mechanism for evolution: random variation sifted by natural selection.

Now, the real problem for Christian theology is that one word, random. Many Christians have thought that natural selection was compatible with their faith because, in the eyes of an infinite God, there is no truly random event. What appears to us as random is nonetheless God's work of creation, planned by Him from all eternity. However, a

---

[4] *Ibid.*

number of people, including some prominent and influential scientists, do not share the Christian, theistic interpretation of Darwin's theory. Many of the leading voices in biology throughout this century have consistently and aggressively proclaimed that Darwin's theory leaves no room for a Creator, because random processes are enough to produce life. In 1959 a large meeting was held at the University of Chicago to celebrate the centenary of the publication of Darwin's *The Origin of Species*. One of the speakers there was Julian Huxley, the grandson of Thomas Henry Huxley, Darwin's contemporary and great defender. In his speech, Huxley proclaimed that

> In the evolutionary pattern of thought there is no longer any need or room for the supernatural. . . . Man is the result of a process that did not have him in mind.[5]

These sentiments persist strongly into our day. Richard Dawkins, an Oxford University professor and well-known popularizer of materialistic Darwinism, has written that "Darwin made it possible to be an intellectually fulfilled atheist."[6] The philosopher Daniel Dennett, in his recent book *Darwin's Dangerous Idea*, compares religious believers to wild animals who may have to be caged, and says that parents should be prevented, presumably by coercion, from misinforming their children about the truth of evolution, which is so evident to him.[7]

Well, of course, professors say silly things all the time; why should we pay any attention to these people? Because, although it is usually couched in more careful phrases, the materialistic interpretation of evolution is the one that

[5] Cited in P.E. Johnson, *Darwin on Trial* (Washington, D.C.: Regnery Gateway, 1991), pp. 150–51.

[6] R. Dawkins, *The Blind Watchmaker* (London: W.W. Norton, 1986), p. 6.

[7] D. Dennett, *Darwin's Dangerous Idea* (New York: Simon & Schuster, 1995), pp. 515–16.

dominates public discussion, and as such it is being taught to many children in the nation's schools. For example, in a well-written high school biology textbook by Miller and Levine, students are told that:

> Of course, there has never been any kind of plan to [evolution] because evolution works without either plan or purpose. . . . It is important to keep this concept in mind: *Evolution is random and undirected.*[8]

In 1995 the National Association of Biology Teachers adopted the following definition of evolutionary theory:

> The diversity of life on earth is the outcome of evolution: an unsupervised, impersonal, unpredictable, and natural process of temporal descent with genetic modification.[9]

More examples could be cited. It is not hard to guess Who they are trying to exclude with words like unsupervised, impersonal, and undirected.

Recall that Pope John Paul II divides a theory of evolution into its mechanism and its philosophy. Now, of course, these statements are philosophy, not science. Science cannot measure plans or purposes or supervision. Nonetheless some scientists and scientific organizations try to attach highly-debatable philosophical baggage to Darwin's mechanism by calling the whole package "science."

Now, it is up to the Church, and to Christian philosophers, theologians, and teachers, to point out the shortcomings of materialistic philosophy. However, it is up to scientists to evaluate any proposed mechanism of evolution. That is what I will focus on in my talk today. I will try to show you why I think, irrespective of the philosophy attached to it, Darwin's mechanism is inadequate to

[8] K.R. Miller and J. Levine, *Biology*, (Englewood Cliffs, New Jersey: Prentice Hall, 1995), p. 658.

[9] National Association of Biology Teachers, "Statement on the Teaching of Evolution" (1995).

explain many aspects of the biological world, especially those discovered in the molecular biological revolution of the past four decades. And I will try to explain why I propose that a better explanation is the intentional design of biological systems by an intelligent agent.

A Series of Eyes

How do we see? In the 19th century the anatomy of the eye was known in great detail and its sophisticated features astounded everyone who was familiar with them. Scientists of the time correctly observed that if a person were so unfortunate as to be missing one of the eye's many integrated features, such as the lens, or iris, or ocular muscles, the inevitable result would be a severe loss of vision or outright blindness. So it was concluded that the eye could only function if it were nearly intact.

Charles Darwin knew about the eye too. In the *Origin of Species* Darwin dealt with many objections to his theory of evolution by natural selection. He discussed the problem of the eye in a section of the book appropriately entitled "Organs of extreme perfection and complication." Somehow, for evolution to be believable, Darwin had to convince the public that complex organs could be formed gradually, in a step-by-step process.

He succeeded brilliantly. Cleverly, Darwin didn't try to discover a real pathway that evolution might have used to make the eye. Instead, he pointed to modern animals with different kinds of eyes, ranging from the simple to the complex, and suggested that the evolution of the human eye might have involved similar organs as intermediates.

Here is a paraphrase of Darwin's argument. Although humans have complex camera-type eyes, many animals get by with less. Some tiny creatures have just a simple group of pigmented cells – not much more than a light sensitive spot. That simple arrangement can hardly be said to confer vision, but it can sense light and dark, and so it meets the creature's needs. The light-sensing organ of some starfishes is somewhat more sophisticated. Their eye is located in a depressed region. This allows the animal to sense which direction the light is coming from, since the curvature of the depression blocks off light from some directions. If the curvature becomes more pronounced, the directional sense of the eye improves. But more curvature lessens the amount of light that enters the eye, decreasing its sensitivity. The sensitivity can be increased by placement of gelatinous material in the cavity to act as a lens. Some modern animals have eyes with such crude lenses. Gradual improvements in the lens could then provide an image of increasing sharpness, as the requirements of the animal's environment dictated.

Using reasoning like this, Darwin convinced many of his readers that an evolutionary pathway leads from the simplest light sensitive spot to the sophisticated camera-eye of man. But the question remains, how did vision begin? Darwin persuaded much of the world that a modern eye evolved gradually from a simpler structure, but he did not even try to explain where his starting point – the 'simple' light sensitive spot – came from. On the contrary, Darwin dismissed the question of the eye's ultimate origin:

> How a nerve comes to be sensitive to light hardly concerns us more than how life itself originated.[10]

He had an excellent reason for declining the question: it was completely beyond nineteenth century science. How the eye works – that is, what happens when a photon of light first hits the retina – simply could not be answered at that time. As a matter of fact, no question about the underlying mechanisms of life could be answered. How did animal muscles cause movement? How did photosynthesis work? How was energy extracted from food? How did the body fight infection? No one knew.

To Darwin vision was a black box, but today, after the hard, cumulative work of many biochemists, we are

[10] C. Darwin, *Origin of Species* (1872) 6th ed. (New York: New York University Press, 1988), p. 151.

approaching answers to the question of sight. To get a flavor of what a theory of evolution must explain let's take Darwin's example of the eye and examine a few of the molecular details of vision that have been discovered by modern science. When light first strikes the retina a photon interacts with a molecule called 11-*cis*-retinal, which rearranges within picoseconds to *trans*-retinal. The change in the shape of retinal forces a change in the shape of the protein, rhodopsin, to which the retinal is tightly bound. The protein's metamorphosis alters its behavior, making it stick to another protein called transducin. Before bumping into activated rhodopsin, transducin had tightly bound a small molecule called GDP. But when transducin interacts with activated rhodopsin, the GDP falls off and a molecule called GTP binds to transducin. (GTP is closely related to, but critically different from, GDP.)

GTP-transducin-activated rhodopsin now binds to a protein called phosphodiesterase, located in the inner membrane of the cell. When attached to activated rhodopsin and its entourage, the phosphodiesterase acquires the ability to chemically cut a molecule called cGMP (a chemical relative of both GDP and GTP). Initially there are a lot of cGMP molecules in the cell, but the phosphodiesterase lowers its concentration, like a pulled plug lowers the water level in a bathtub.

Another membrane protein that binds cGMP is called an ion channel. It acts as a gateway that regulates the number of sodium ions in the cell. Normally the ion channel allows sodium ions to flow into the cell, while a separate protein actively pumps them out again. The dual action of the ion channel and pump keeps the level of sodium ions in the cell within a narrow range. When the amount of cGMP is reduced because of cleavage by the phosphodiesterase, the ion channel closes, causing the cellular concentration of positively charged sodium ions to be reduced. This causes an imbalance of charge across the cell membrane which, finally, causes a current to be transmitted down the optic nerve to the brain. The result, when interpreted by the brain, is vision.

This description is just a sketchy overview of the biochemistry of vision. Ultimately, though, *this* is what it means to "explain" vision. *This* is the level of explanation for which biological science must aim. In order to truly understand a function, one must understand in detail every relevant step in the process. The relevant steps in biological processes occur ultimately at the molecular level, so a satisfactory explanation of a biological phenomenon – such as vision, or digestion, or immunity – must include its molecular explanation.

Now that the black box of vision has been opened it is no longer enough for an "evolutionary explanation" of that power to consider only the *anatomical* structures of whole eyes, as Darwin did in the nineteenth century, and as popularizers of evolution continue to do today. Each of the anatomical steps and structures that Darwin thought were so simple actually involves staggeringly complicated biochemical processes that cannot be papered over with rhetoric. The details of life are handled by molecular machines. Darwin's theory will stand or fall on its ability to explain *them*.

Irreducible Complexity

So how can we decide if Darwin's theory can account for the complexity of molecular life? It turns out that Darwin himself set a standard. He acknowledged that:

> If it could be demonstrated that any complex organ existed which could not possibly have been formed by numerous, successive, slight modifications, my theory would absolutely break down.[11]

But what type of biological system could not be formed by "numerous, successive, slight modifications"?

[11] Darwin, Ibid., p. 154.

Well, for starters, a system is *irreducibly complex*. By this I mean that the system is composed of several interacting parts, and where the removal of any one of the parts causes the system to cease functioning.

Let's consider an everyday example of irreducible complexity: the humble mousetrap. The mousetraps that my family uses consist of a number of parts. There are: 1) a flat wooden platform to act as a base; 2) a metal hammer, which does the actual job of crushing the little mouse; 3) a spring with extended ends to press against the platform and the hammer when the trap is charged; 4) a sensitive catch which releases when slight pressure is applied, and 5) a metal bar which connects to the catch and holds the hammer back when the trap is charged. Now you can't catch a mouse with just a platform, add a spring and catch a few more mice, add a holding bar and catch a few more. All the pieces of the mousetrap have to be in place before you catch any mice. Therefore the mousetrap is irreducibly complex.

An irreducibly complex system cannot be produced directly by numerous, successive, slight modifications of a precursor system, because any precursor to an irreducibly complex system that is missing a part is by definition non-functional. An irreducibly complex biological system, if there is such a thing, would be a powerful challenge to Darwinian evolution. Since natural selection can only choose systems that are already working, then if a biological system cannot be produced gradually it would have to arise as an integrated unit for natural selection to have anything to act on.

Let me add a word of caution. Demonstration that a system is irreducibly complex is not a proof that there is absolutely no gradual route to its production. Although an irreducibly complex system can't be produced directly, one can't definitively rule out the possibility of an indirect, circuitous route. However, as the complexity of an interacting system increases, the likelihood of such an indirect route drops precipitously. And as the number of unexplained, irreducibly complex biological systems increases, our con-

fidence that Darwin's criterion of failure has been met sky-
rockets toward the maximum that science allows.

The Cilium

Now, mousetraps are one thing, biochemical systems are
another. So we must ask, are any biochemical systems irreducibly complex? Yes, it turns out that many are. A good
example is the cilium. Cilia are hairlike structures on the
surfaces of many animal and lower plant cells that can
move fluid over the cell's surface or "row" single cells
through a fluid. In humans, for example, cells lining the
respiratory tract each have about 200 cilia that beat in syn-
chrony to sweep mucus towards the throat for elimination.
What is the structure of a cilium? A cilium consists of a bun-
dle of fibers called an axoneme. An axoneme contains a
ring of 9 double "microtubules" surrounding two central
single microtubules. Each outer doublet consists of a ring of
13 filaments (subfiber A) fused to an assembly of 10 filaments (subfiber B). The filaments of the microtubules are
composed of two proteins called alpha and beta tubulin.
The 11 microtubules forming an axoneme are held together
by three types of connectors: subfibers A are joined to the
central microtubules by radial spokes; adjacent outer dou-
blets are joined by linkers of a highly elastic protein called
nexin; and the central microtubules are joined by a con-
necting bridge. Finally, every subfiber A bears two arms, an
inner arm and an outer arm, both containing a protein
called dynein.

Although even this seems complex, a brief description
can't do justice to the full complexity of the cilium, which
has been shown by biochemical analysis to contain about
200 separate kinds of protein parts.

But how does a cilium work? Experiments have shown
that ciliary motion results from the chemically-powered
"walking" of the dynein arms on one microtubule up a second microtubule so that the two microtubules slide past
each other. The protein cross-links between microtubules in
a cilium prevent neighboring microtubules from sliding

past each other by more than a short distance. These cross-links, therefore, convert the dynein-induced sliding motion to a bending motion of the entire axoneme.

Now, let us consider what this implies. What components are needed for a cilium to work? Ciliary motion certainly requires microtubules; otherwise, there would be no strands to slide. Additionally we require a motor, or else the microtubules of the cilium would lie stiff and motionless. Furthermore, we require linkers to tug on neighboring strands, converting the sliding motion into a bending motion, and preventing the structure from falling apart. All of these parts are required to perform one function: ciliary motion. Just as a mousetrap does not work unless all of its constituent parts are present, ciliary motion simply does not exist in the absence of microtubules, connectors, and motors. Therefore, we can conclude that the cilium is irreducibly complex – an enormous monkey wrench thrown into its presumed gradual, Darwinian evolution.

Another Example

Another example of irreducible complexity is the system that targets proteins for delivery to subcellular compartments. The eukaryotic cell contains a number of subcellular compartments to perform specialized tasks, like rooms in a house. These include lysosomes for digestion, Golgi vesicles for export, and others. Unfortunately, the machinery for making proteins is outside these compartments, so how do the proteins which perform tasks in subcellular compartments find their way to their destination? It turns out that proteins that will wind up in subcellular compartments contain a special amino acid sequence near the beginning called a "signal sequence." As the proteins are being synthesized, a complex molecular assemblage called the signal recognition particle or SRP, binds to the signal sequence. This causes synthesis of the protein to halt temporarily. During the pause in protein synthesis the SRP binds the trans-membrane SRP receptor, which causes protein synthesis to resume and which allows passage of the protein into the interior of the endoplasmic reticulum (ER). As the protein passes into the ER the signal sequence is cut off.

For many proteins the ER is just a waystation on their travels to their final destinations. Proteins which will end up in a lysosome are enzymatically "tagged" with a carbohydrate residue called mannose-6-phosphate while still in the ER. An area of the ER membrane then begins to concentrate several proteins; one protein, clathrin, forms a sort of geodesic dome called a coated vesicle which buds off from the ER. In the dome there is also a receptor protein which binds to both the clathrin and to the mannose-6-phosphate group of the protein which is being transported. The coated vesicle then leaves the ER, travels through the cytoplasm, and binds to the lysosome through another specific receptor protein. Finally, in a maneuver involving several more proteins, the vesicle fuses with the lysosome and the protein is at its destination.

During its travels our protein interacted with dozens of macromolecules to achieve one purpose: its arrival in the lysosome. Virtually all components of the transport system are necessary for the system to operate, and therefore the system is irreducible. The consequences of a gap in the transport chain can be seen in the hereditary defect known as I-cell disease. It results from a deficiency of the enzyme that places the mannose-6-phosphate on proteins to be targeted to the lysosomes. I-cell disease is characterized by progressive retardation, skeletal deformities, and early death.

The Professional Literature

There are many other examples of irreducibly complex biochemical systems, including aspects of blood clotting, the bacterial flagellum, telomeres, photosynthesis, transcription regulation, and much more. Examples of irreducible complexity can be found on virtually every page of a biochemistry textbook. But if, as I contend, these things cannot be explained by Darwinian evolution, how has the scientific community dealt with these phenomena over the past forty years?

A good place to see how science has dealt with the origin of biochemical systems is in the *Journal of Molecular Evolution*. *JME* is a journal that was begun specifically to deal with the topic of how evolution occurs on the molecular level. It has high scientific standards, and is edited by prominent figures in the field. In a recent issue of *JME* there were published eleven articles; of these, all eleven were concerned simply with the comparison of protein or DNA sequences. A sequence comparison is an amino acid-by-amino acid comparison of two different proteins, or a nucleotide-by-nucleotide comparison of two different pieces of DNA, noting the positions at which they are identical or similar, and the places where they are not. Although useful for determining possible lines of descent, which is an interesting question in its own right, merely comparing sequences cannot show how a complex biochemical system achieved its function – the question that most concerns us here. By way of analogy, the instruction manuals for two different models of computer put out by the same company might have many identical words, sentences, and even paragraphs, suggesting a common ancestry (perhaps the same author wrote both manuals), but comparing the sequences of letters in the instruction manuals will never tell us if a computer can be produced step by step starting from a typewriter.

None of the papers discussed detailed models for intermediates in the development of complex biomolecular structures. In the past ten years *JME* has published over a thousand papers. Of these, about one hundred discussed the chemical synthesis of molecules thought to be necessary for the origin of life, about 50 proposed mathematical models to improve sequence analysis, and about 800 were analyses of sequences. There were no papers discussing detailed models for intermediates in the development of complex biomolecular structures. This is not what you would expect from a journal with such a name. *JME*'s silence is indicative of the biochemical literature as a whole. *No* journal contains much in the way of explanations for the production of irreducibly complex biochemical structures by natural selection.

Acculturation

In my experience many scientists are skeptical that Darwinian mechanisms can explain all of life. However, a large number do believe it. Since the professional biochemical literature contains no detailed explanations of how complex systems might have arisen, why is Darwinism nonetheless credible with many biochemists? A large part of the answer is a sociological one: they have been taught as part of their biochemical training that Darwinism is true. To understand both the success of Darwinism as orthodoxy and its failure as science at the molecular level let's briefly examine the textbooks that are used to teach aspiring scientists.

A good place to find out the real importance of Darwinian evolution to the understanding of life is a biochemistry textbook's index. An index lists all the subjects covered in the book, and the number of citations is a rough measure of the subject's importance. A survey of thirty biochemistry textbooks used in major universities over the past generation shows that many textbooks ignore evolution completely. For example, Thomas Devlin of Jefferson University wrote a biochemistry textbook that has gone through three editions. The first edition has about 2500 entries in its index, the second also has 2500, and the third has 5000. But none refer to evolution. A textbook by Frank Armstrong of North Carolina State University, published by Oxford University Press, is the only recent book to include an historical chapter reviewing important developments in biochemistry, beginning with the synthesis of urea by Friedrich Wöhler in 1828. The chapter does not mention Darwin or evolution. In three editions Armstrong's book has found it unnecessary to mention evolution in its index. Another textbook published by John Wiley & Sons has one citation to evolution in its index out of a total of about 2500. It refers to a sentence on page 4: "Organisms have evolved and adapted to changing conditions on a geological time scale and continue to do so."[12] Nothing else is said.

Despite having little to say about how specific molecular systems may have evolved by Darwinian means, some textbooks make a concerted effort to acculturate students to an evolutionary view of the world. For example, a bio-chemistry textbook by Voet & Voet contains a marvelous, full-color drawing nicely capturing the orthodox position.[13] The top third of the drawing shows a volcano, lightning, an ocean, and little rays of sunlight, to suggest how life start-ed. The middle of the picture has a stylized drawing of a DNA molecule leading out from the origin of life ocean and into a bacterial cell, to show how life developed. The bot-tom third of the picture – no kidding – is like the Garden of Eden, depicting a number of animals that have been pro-duced by evolution milling about. Included in the throng are a man and a woman (the woman is offering the man an apple), both especially attractive and in the buff. This undoubtedly adds to the interest for students, but the drawing is a tease. The implicit promise that the secrets of evolution will be uncovered is never consummated Many students learn from their textbooks how to view the world through an evolutionary lens. However, they do not learn how Darwinian evolution might have produced any of the remarkably intricate biochemical systems that those texts describe.

Because he was unaware of the basis of life, Darwin had to appeal to the imagination of his readers to come up with possible evolutionary pathways. But imagination is a two-edged sword. An imaginative person might see things that

[12] E.E. Conn, P.K. Stumpf, G. Bruening, and R.H. Doi, *Outlines of Biochemistry*, 5th ed. (New York: John Wiley & Sons, 1985), p. 4.

[13] D. Voet and J.G. Voet, *Biochemistry*, 2nd ed. (New York: John Wiley & Sons, 1995), p. 19.

other people miss, or he might see things that aren't there. For science, imagination is a wonderful place to start, but it is a terrible place to end. A review of the science literature shows that Darwin's theory has become stuck in the world of imagination.

Detection of Design

So far my criticisms of evolution are not much different from what a number of other scientists have offered. The shortcomings of Darwinian explanations have been noted by Stuart Kauffman, Lynn Margulis, Brian Goodwin, James Shapiro, and others. Where I differ from the other critics, however, is in the conclusion I draw from the complexity of cellular systems. I argue that the systems show strong evidence of design – purposeful, intentional design by an intelligent agent. I think it is safe to say that it is the conclusion of design, much more than my criticism of Darwinism, that has attracted attention. So let's look at the idea of design.

What is "design"? Design is simply the *purposeful arrangement of parts*. With such a broad definition its is easy to see that anything *might* have been designed. The coats on a rack in a restaurant may have been arranged just-so by the owner before you came in. The trash and tin cans along the edge of a highway may have been placed by an artist trying to make some obscure environmental statement. On the campus of my university there are sculptures which, if I saw them lying beside the road, I would guess were the result of chance blows to a piece of scrap metal, but they were designed.

The upshot of this conclusion – that anything *could* have been purposely arranged – is that we can never positively rule out design. Nonetheless, it is a good rule of thumb to assume there is no design unless one can detect it. The scientific problem then becomes, how do we confidently *detect* design? When is it reasonable to conclude, in the absence of firsthand knowledge or eyewitness accounts, that something has been designed?

There are several ways to detect design. However, for discrete physical systems design is most easily apprehended when a number of separate, interacting components are ordered in such a way as to accomplish a function beyond the individual components. To illustrate, consider a Far Side cartoon by Gary Larson in which an exploring team is going through a jungle, and the lead explorer has been strung up and skewered. A companion turns to another and confides, "That's why I never walk in front." Now every person who sees the cartoon immediately knows that the trap was *designed*. In fact, Larson's humor depends on you recognizing the design. It wouldn't be terribly funny if the first explorer had just fallen off a cliff or a rotted tree accidentally fell on him. No, his fate was intended. But how do you know that? How does the audience apprehend that this trap was designed? You can tell that the trap was designed because of the way the parts interact with great specificity to perform a function. Like the mousetrap we saw in the beginning of the talk, no one would mistake the cartoon system for an accidental arrangement of parts. Further, all of the parts of the trap are natural components: a vine, a tree, some pieces of wood. There are no artificial, manufactured pieces. Therefore, we can come to a conclusion of design for a system composed entirely of natural parts.

Let's ask a few more questions about the Far Side situation. When was the trap made? Just from looking at it, you can't tell if the trap was put together an hour ago, last week, or last year. Although by gathering further evidence you might be able to narrow down that question (for instance, by noting that twenty years ago the tree would not have been tall enough to support the trap) the point I wish to make here is that we apprehend design independently of knowing when the design took place. As a matter of fact, we must first recognize that there has been a design event be fore we can even entertain the question of when the event took place.

Who made the trap? We might guess that perhaps a resident of the jungle constructed it to defend his homeland. However, suppose over a bottle of wine later in the evening one of the other explorers confesses that he made the trap, stealing away from camp one night last month and constructing it along a path that he knew the group would later be taking. Just by looking at the trap, you can't tell who made it. Either of these possibilities is consistent with the appearance of the trap. The identity of the designer is a separate question which doesn't even arise until we apprehend that a system was designed.

Let's push this thought a little further. Where is the trap? We see it's in a jungle somewhere, but where? Suppose we were told that these folks are actually space explorers, and that they are the first people ever to land on an alien planet, light years from earth. They are exploring an alien jungle when the unfortunate lead explorer is skewered. Now, who designed the trap? Was it a member of the space party? Was it an intelligent alien? Although we can tell that the trap was designed, we cannot determine the designer's identity simply by looking at the trap. The conclusion I wish to draw here is that we can apprehend design without knowing who the designer is.

With these preliminary questions cleared out of the way I suggest that many biochemical systems were designed by an intelligent agent. Our ability to be confident of the design of the cilium or intracellular transport rests on the same principles as our ability to be confident of the design of the jungle trap: the ordering of separate components to achieve an identifiable function that depends sharply on the components.

Who did the designing, when, where, and how, remain open questions that may or may not be accessible to science. But the fact of design itself can be deduced from the structure of the systems which biochemists have elucidated in the past decades.

Reception of the Book

My book has been out for about eight months now,

enough time for reaction to it to come in from various corners. I think it's safe to say that the reaction has been mixed. A number of reviews have been quite favorable, and a number unfavorable. Let's take a minute to see what has been said in reviews of the book by other biologists. First of all, in all the reviews of my book that I am aware of, no one claims that the biochemical systems I describe have already been explained by science. James Shreeve, reviewing the book for the *New York Times* says "Mr. Behe may be right that given our current state of knowledge, good old Darwinian evolution cannot explain the origin of blood clotting or cellular transport." In *National Review* microbiologist James Shapiro of the University of Chicago writes "There are no detailed Darwinian accounts for the evolution of any fundamental biochemical or cellular system, only a variety of wishful speculations." In *Nature* University of Chicago evolutionary biologist Jerry Coyne, although very unfriendly to the concept of intelligent design, states "There is no doubt that the pathways described by Behe are dauntingly complex, and their evolution will be hard to unravel. . . . We may forever be unable to envisage the first proto-pathways." In *New Scientist* Andrew Pomiankowski writes, "Pick up any biochemistry textbook, and you will find perhaps two or three references to evolution. Turn to one of these and you will be lucky to find anything better than 'evolution selects the fittest molecules for their biological function.'" So apparently everyone at least agrees that complex biochemical systems have yet to be explained.

However, none of the reviewers are willing to come to the conclusion of intelligent design. Here are their reasons:

> " Shouldn't we leave something for our children and grandchildren to puzzle out besides which systems in the cell are intelligently designed and which are not? Because something is beyond our understanding today does not mean it will be beyond theirs."
>
> James Shreeve, *New York Times Book Review*

" Sadly, despite its valuable critique of an all-too-often unchallenged orthodoxy, *Darwin's Black Box* fails to capture the true excitement of contemporary biology because it is fighting the battles of the past rather than seeing the vision of the future."

James Shapiro, *National Review*

" It is not valid, however, to assume that, because one man cannot imagine such pathways, they could not have existed."

Jerry Coyne, *Nature*

" So what we have here is just the latest, and no doubt not the last, attempt to put God back into nature."

Andrew Pomiankowski, *New Scientist*

It is clear from the quotations, I think, that the reviewers are not rejecting design because there is scientific evidence against it, or because it violates some principle of logic. Rather, I believe they find design unacceptable because they are uncomfortable with the theological ramifications of the theory. This viewpoint was expressed very clearly recently by the biologist Richard Lewontin. In a review of Carl Sagan's last book in the *New York Review* Lewontin wrote:

> Our willingness to accept scientific claims that are against common sense is the key to an understanding of the real struggle between science and the supernatural. We take the side of science in spite of the patent absurdity of some of its constructs, . . . in spite of the tolerance of the scientific community for unsubstantiated just-so stories, because we have a prior commitment, a commitment to materialism.[14]

Pope John Paul II noted that a theory of evolution has

[14] R. Lewontin, "Billions and Billions of Demons," *New York Review of Books* (January 9, 1997), p.

two parts, the mechanism and the philosophy attached to that mechanism. Putting it like that, however, makes it sound as if any philosophy can be mixed and matched with any mechanism. But the situation is not really that clean cut. While Catholics and theists in general can accommodate the mechanism of Darwin to their worldview, materialists *require* something like Darwinism because, ultimately, materialism says that life and intelligence had to arise unaided from brute matter. A theory of intelligent design, however, holds implicitly that there is a designer capable of planning and executing the phenomenal intricacies of life on earth. Although there are, at least in theory, some exotic candidates for the role of designer that might be compatible with materialist philosophy (such as space aliens or time travelers), few people will be convinced by these, and will conclude that the designer is beyond nature. Many scientists are unable or unwilling to accept such a designer, because that goes against their prior commitment to materialism, or at least to a functional materialism in the course of their work.

Nonetheless I remain optimistic that the scientific community will eventually come around to accepting intelligent design, even if the acceptance is discreet and muted. The reason for optimism is the advance of science itself, which almost every day discovers new intricacies in nature, fresh reasons for recognizing the design inherent to life and the universe.

In the meantime, there is nothing to stop nonscientists from recognizing and appreciating that design. We are fearfully and wonderfully made, and every cell of our bodies testifies to the intelligence that pervades creation.

FAITH AND THE STRUCTURE OF THE COSMOS

Stephen M. Barr

I. Introduction

I have been asked to talk about "faith and the structure of the cosmos." That is a large subject indeed, and there is far more to say about it, se, than I can say in 45 minutes. I am therefore going to have narrow my focus a little, and concentrate on only one aspect of the relationship between faith and cosmology. I am going to talk about a subject that has attracted a lot of attention in recent years: "anthropic coincidences" and the Anthropic Principle.

The term "anthropic coincidences" refers to the fact that certain features of the laws of physics seem to be arranged in such a way as to make possible the emergence of life in our universe. The word "anthropic" has been objected to by some people on the ground that most coincidences that have been studied pertain to the possibility of life in a fairly broad sense, rather than intelligent life or specifically human life. Nevertheless, without these "coincidences" we would not be here, and therefore it is fair to take them as evidence that we human beings were meant to be here, that we were built in to the very structure of the cosmos. This would bear out the traditional Jewish and Christian belief that the universe was largely created for our sakes. This belief is stated, for instance, in The Epistle to Diognetus, written in the second century, which says, "God loved the race of men. It was for their sakes that He made the world." Conceivably, there are other races of intelligent and free creatures somewhere in the cosmos. If so, then they too have spiritual souls, and one presumes that the cosmos was made as much for them as for us.

The idea of "anthropic coincidences" should not be confused with the so-called "Anthropic Principle." Anthropic coincidences are certain facts about the universe; the Anthropic Principle is a highly speculative hypothesis which may be a way of explaining some of these facts without invoking God. I will discuss the Anthropic le in the last part of my talk.

I would like to give a number examples of anthropic coincidences, but before doing so it may be helpful to introduce a few basic facts and a bit of terminology.

The first fact is that there are four basic forces of nature known at the present. They are gravity, electromagnetism, the weak nuclear force, and the strong nuclear force. The second fact is that an atom consists of a cloud of electrons orbiting a small dense clump called a nucleus. The plural of nucleus is nuclei pronounced NU-CLEE-EYE by physicists). Nuclei are, in turn, made up of particles called "nucleons". Nucleons come in two types: protons and neutrons. The third fact is that the nucleons are held together inside a nucleus by the strong force. And the fourth and last fact is that atomic nuclei were forged or synthesized in three places: the fires of the Big Bang, the interiors of stars, and the explosions, called supernovas, in which some stars end their lives. The forging of the atomic nuclei, called "nucleosynthesis," is a step-by-step process. It begins with individual nucleons, which then combine together into larger and larger nuclei. The smallest nucleus is that of ordinary hydrogen which consists of just a single proton. The largest naturally occurring nucleus is uranium, which has 92 protons and an even larger number of neutrons. Notice that if you know how many protons a nucleus has, then you know what kind of atom it is the nucleus of – i.e. which chemical element it is. For example, a nucleus which has six protons in it, and however many neutron, is a nucleus of carbon. So, when one discusses nucleosynthesis, one is discussing the origin of the chemical elements. The reason that I have focused on the origin of the elements is simply that one seems to need a rich variety of chemical elements to make living things. The human body contains at least twenty five different chemical elements.

That is about all you need to know. Now let me give me a few examples on anthropic coincidences.

II. Some examples of anthropic coincidences

Example #1: The first step in making the elements, that is in nucleosynthesis, is to make a nucleus which has two nucleons in it. There is only one such nucleus, call "deuterium," and it is made up proton and one neutron. The making of deuterium is the first rung on the ladder of nucleosynthesis. Deuterium, as it happens, is a very held-together nucleus. It just barely makes it. It has been estimated that if the strong force were only about ten percent weaker than it is, a proton and neutron would not be able to stick together at all. Nucleosythesis would be completely stymied. There would be no nuclei that had two or more nucleons in them. That is, the only chemical element that would exist in Nature would be ordinary hydrogen, which, as I have said, has a nucleus consisting only of a single proton. Having no elements other than hydrogen would surely preclude the emergence of life – at least life that is based on chemistry. Moreover, the nuclear fusion reactions that make stars shine would also be impossible.

On the other hand, if the nuclear force were only a few percent stronger is, the opposite disaster would occur. Then not only would deuteroium exist, but a new kind nucleus, made up of two protons and helium-2, would be able to exist also. In that case, all the hydrogen nuclei in the universe would have paired together in the Big Bang to make helium-2 nuclei. There would be virtually no hydrogen left. That, as Prof. Behe can tell you, would be an utter disaster for biology, since virtually all organic compounds contain hydrogen. Moreover, hydrogen nuclei are the main nuclear fuel of stars like the sun. Thus, the strength of the nuclear force has just the right value to allow life as we know it: a few percent weaker or a few percent stronger and we would not be here.

Example #2: The second important step in nucleosynthesis is that two deuterium nuclei combine to make helium-4, which has two protons and two neutrons. This step is easy, and a lot of helium-4 is made both in the Big Bang and in the stars. But the step after that is extraordinarily difficult, and in fact would not happen to any significant degree except for another remarkable coincidence in the laws of nature. The problem is that four nucleons are very happy being bound together into a helium-4 nucleus. They form a sort of exclusive club. In fact, they have a special name: a helium-4 nucleus is also called an "alpha" particle, for historical reasons that we needn't go into. So, if a fifth nucleon comes along and tries to join the club, it is rejected. Similarly, if two helium-4's – i.e. two alphas – try to get together, they fail. They would rather stay as two alphas. So there is a terrible bottleneck problem: how does anything bigger than helium-4 ever get put together?

The answer is the following. Inside a star helium-4 nuclei are constantly into each other. When they do, they can stick together very briefly for about a hundred millionth of a billionth of a second. In that brief moment it can happen that a third helium-4 nucleus comes along and hits them. If that happens the three helium-4 nuclei can fuse together to form a carbon-12 nucleus. This is called the "three-alpha process." Once carbon has been produced in this way, everything proceeds smoothly in building up all the larger elements. For example, carbon-12 has no problem joining up with another helium-4 to make an oxygen-16 nucleus.

Now, as you might imagine, this three-alpha process is a tricky thing. You don't often get a third helium-4 just happening to come along in that hundred millionth of a billionth of a second when it is needed. And the physicists first did calculations estimating how much carbon would be produced in this way in stars, it seemed that much less would be made than actually exists in Nature. They were baffled. Then Fred Hoyle, the famous astrophysicist, suggested that the three-alpha process might be enhanced by something called a "resonance." Resonances are an important phenomenon in physics. There are many examples or them in everyday life. When a big truck goes by, the noise of the truck can make the window panes start rattling very strongly, if one of the natural "modes of vibration" of the windows just happens to match up with the frequency of the sound. Or, you have heard of how opera singers are supposed to be able to shatter wine glasses by hitting just the right note. In other words, an effect that would ordinarily be a very weak one, can be greatly enhanced if it happens "resonantly". Well, atomic nuclei also have characteristic "notes" or "modes of vibration" called "energy levels," and nuclear reactions can be enormously facilitated if they happen to hit on one of them.

So Fred Hoyle pointed out that if the carbon-12 nucleus has an energy level injust the right place, then the three alpha process can be enhanced enough to make the amount of carbon that we see. And, lo and behold, when nuclear physicists went to their labs and studied carbon-12 nuclei, they found an energy level just exactly where it was needed. If it had been a few percent higher or lower in frequency it would not have enhanced the three- alpha process, and there would be very little of carbon or the heavier elements around in the universe. Life as we know it would not have been able to exist. Our existence depends on that fragile coincidence.

Example 3: Now, let us turn from the strong force to the electromagnetic force. The electromagnetic force is about a hundred times weaker than the strong force. And this is closely connected with the fact that there are about a hundred types of elements in nature. The point is that atomic nuclei are held together by the strong force, but at the same time, the protons in the nucleus, because they all have positive electric charge, are repelling each other electrically and straining mightily to get out. If the number of protons in a nucleus is too large, then the electric repulsion over-powers the strong force and the nucleus disintegrates. That is why uranium, for example, which has 92 protons in it, is unstable to being fissioned. If the electric force were much stronger than it actually is in our universe, then only very small nuclei would be a able to exist without disintegrating in this way. There would be very few kinds of chemicals, and that would be bad for making life. In fact, here would be a number of other disasters as well if the electromagnet-ic force were much stronger than it is. For example, isolat-ed protons would be unstable, and as a result no ordinary hydrogen would exist in Nature. I have already explained why that would be disastrous.

Example 4: Another fortunate fact has to do with the flat-ness of space. Einstein taught us that space (or rather space-time) is not flat, but curved. Because of this curvature, bod-ies seem to attract each other by the force we call gravity. However, it turns out that the space of our universe, if looked at on large scales of distance, is astonishingly flat on the average. The "spatial curvature," as it is called, is very small. In fact, shortly after the Big Bang the spatial curva-ture of the universe was zero to many, many decimal places. For a long time, this was called the "flatness prob-lem," because no one could think of a good explanation for it. We now do have a good explanation called "cosmic infla-tion." But the point of interest to us at the moment is that if the flatness of space had not been fantastically small to begin with the universe would either have come to an end after a very short time – a small fraction of a second – or would have expanded so rapidly that the universe would be too cold and empty for stars and life to appear.

Example #5: So far I have talked about various quanti-ties, like the strength of the strong and electromagnetic forces, and the flatness of space, which have to have very special numerical values if life as we know it were to be possible. But there are also certain gross qualitative features of the laws of physics that are very important in making life possible. One example is the fact that the number of space dimensions is three. If we lived in a world with four or more space dimensions, the gravitational force between two objects would depend in a different way on the distance between two objects would depend in a different way on the distance between the objects. It can be shown that the orbits of planets would be unstable and wildly erratic. Planets would go rapidly from being very close to their stars to being very far away. Temperatures on planets would oscillate between extremes, with disastrous consequences. It has been argued that atoms would collapse by having their electrons plunge into their nuclei. On the other hand, if there were fewer than three space dimensions, complex organisms would probably be impossible. In particular, complex wiring, as is needed in a brain, is not possible in one or two dimensions. If one tries to draw complicated wiring diagrams on a two-dimensional surface, one finds that the wires have to cross each other many times, which would lead to short-circuits.

Example #6: My last example is the fact that nature obeys the principles of quantum theory. It turns out that matter would not be stable in a non-quantum world. What ultimately is responsible for the fact that particles form stable atoms with well-defined chemical properties is the Heisenberg Uncertainty Principle.

I will stop here, although I could give dozens of even more striking examples of features of our world, that could have been different, and lay an important role in making the existence of life possible. I should interject a word of warning here, however. Even though there many genuine anthropic coincidences, there are some authors out there who make reckless and even wild claims about them.

What do physicists say about anthropic coincidences? There is a wide spectrum of opinion. Quite a number of the greatest scientists of our time, such as Ya Zel'dovich, Andrei Sakharov, Lev Okun, Martin Rees, and Steven Weinberg, to mention just a few, have been interested in them and have devoted study to them. However, there is also a widespread feeling of skepticism in the physics community and even in many cases extreme hostility to the very idea of anthropic coincidences. Part of this skepticism has to do with the fact that discussions of anthropic coincidences smack of teleology, and physicists have a strong, instinctive, professional aversion to teleological thinking. The scientific revolution was to a large extent made possible by the rejection of teleological thinking about the physical world in favor of mechanistic thinking. To be honest, however, it is not just teleology that some scientists smell, it is religion.

But aside from merely visceral reactions, there are several arguments that are made against the idea that we can meaningfully talk about anthropic coincidences at all. Let me discuss the three arguments that I know about.

III. Objections to the very idea of anthropic coincidences.

First, there is the argument that we cannot really know what is necessary for life to arise. Life might take forms that are utterly alien to our experience. While the life that we know about makes use of a certain kind of physics, who knows whether with different physical laws completely different possibilities for life might have existed?

This objection has some real force. In most cases, I think that all we can honestly assert is that it appears very unlikely that life could have risen had the laws of physics been different in this or that respect – unlikely, but perhaps not utterly impossible. In these questions, absolute certainty may not be attainable. Nevertheless, I think that we will have achieved something quite significant if we are able to say that there are strong reasons to believe that the cosmos was made with us in mind even if those reasons do not add up to an absolutely rigorous proof.

The second objection is that conventional scientific explanations may exist for some if not all of the facts that now appear as anthropic coincidences. In fact, among the six examples I chose of anthropic coincidences I deliberately included two where we may already have at least a partial explanation of the fact involved. The fact that the electromagnetic force is much weaker than the strong nuclear force, which was my third example, is probably partly explained by the idea of "grand unification." There are reasons to believe that the electromagnetic, weak, and strong forces are really aspects of one underlying "grand unified" force. If that is so, then the strengths of the different forces are not independent of each other, but are tied together in some way. In a typical grand unified model, in fact – and many such models have been proposed – the electromagnetic force does indeed come out to be much weaker than the strong nuclear force.

Similarly, the flatness of space, which was my fourth example, is very likely to be explained as being the result of a phenomenon called cosmic "inflation," which I have already referred to but which unfortunately I haven't time to go into here.

Thus, some or many of the facts about the laws of physics that appear favorable to our existence may have conventional scientific explanations. However, even if that were true of all the coincidences, it would not explain those coincidences away. The critical point was well expressed by the astrophysicists Carr and Rees:

> "One day we may have a more physical explanation for some of the relationships . . . that now seem genuine coincidences. For example, the coincidence [relating the strength of the gravitational force to the strength of the weak force] which is essential for [nucleosynthesis], may eventually be subsumed as a consequence of some presently unformulated unified theory. However, even if all apparently anthropic coincidences could be plained in this way, it would still be remarkable that the relationships dictated by physical theory happened also to be those propitious for life."

In other words, suppose that there are fifteen numerical relationships that have to hold in order for life to be possible, and suppose that in some physical theory all of those very same fifteen relationships happen to hold as a consequence of some underlying physical principle. That would itself be an astonishing set of coincidences.

This brings us to the third objection, which is closely related to the second. Some would say that "God had no choice." In other words, all relationships in Nature are dictated by some deep underlying principles that leave no room for things to have been done differently. Some people even suggest that the laws of nature may be somehow unique. Everything about the physical world – the kinds of particles that exist, the kinds of forces and their relative strengths, the number of dimensions of space and its degree of flatness, the energy levels of the carbon-12 nucleus, and so on, down to the smallest detail – are all what they are because they have to be so. Some physical principle requires it. So God could not have arranged things to achieve conditions "propitious for life," since he had no freedom in arranging things at all. Some deep physical principle or principles tied his hands.

However, this is clearly wrong. There was always the choice of what physical principles to use in constructing the universe. Let me give an example. We saw that it was a lucky thing for the prospects for life that the electromagnetic force is relatively a weak one. And it is true that within the framework of grand unified theories that weakness of electromagnetism arises as a consequence of certain deeper principles. However, it was not necessarily that the world be built along the lines of a grand unified theory. In fact, we do not yet know whether or not it is. So God had a choice in the matter – in fact, many choices, since there are many mathematically consistent grand unified theories, and many equally consistent non-unified theories, and many equally consistent non-unified theories.

The fact is that there are an infinite number of mathematically self-consistent sets of laws of physics that could have been chosen as the basis for the structure of our universe. This fact is absolutely undeniable. Why, then, do some very good physicists talk about the laws of physics possibly being "unique"? What they have in mind is the fact that if certain conditions are imposed upon nature, then there may be a mathematically unique way of satisfying those conditions. For example, if the laws of physics have to satisfy the principles of quantum theory, and also have to contain Einstein's theory of gravity, then they may have to have a unique form. It may well be that there is only one mathematically consistent way to combine Einstein's theory of gravity with quantum theory. However, who said that the universe had to satisfy either quantum principles or contain Einsteinian gravity? When some physicists talk about the laws of physics possibly being unique, what they really mean to say is that the structure of those laws may be uniquely determined once some particular conditions on the nature of the physical world have been assumed to hold.

In short, the universe could have been made differently, and if it had been life might not have been able to arise. These assertions can hardly be contested.

IV. Weak Anthropic Principle.

Now, there is a way to explain the fact that there are anthropic coincidences which does not invoke God. It is called the Weak Anthropic Principle. There are various Anthropic Principles around; some of them are pretty silly. The only one that is really worthy of consideration is the Weak Anthropic Principle. The best way to explain it is by an analogy.

There many things about conditions on the earth that are propitious for life. If the earth were much smaller, then it would not be able to retain an atmosphere. If it were much bigger, it would retain a lot of hydrogen in its atmosphere, which might be bad for life. If it were much closer to the sun it would be too hot to have liquid water, if much farther away it would be too cold. Has someone "fine-tuned" conditions here to make life possible? Not necessarily. There are, after all a vast number of planets in the universe. At least, we may presume that there are. (In fact, it is not unlikely that there are an infinite number). Some planets will be hot, and some cold. Some will be big, and some small. Indeed, they will span a huge range of physical and chemical conditions. Therefore, it is inevitable that some of them will fall into the range where life is possible. Someone might be tempted to ask why we happen to live on such a planet. But obviously that is no coincidence. Life will only arise on those exceptional planets where the conditions are just right to allow it.

To put it another way, if I try one key in an unknown lock, it would be an astonishing coincidence if it worked. But if I try a million keys it would not be greatly surprising if one happened to work.

Now the idea of the Weak Anthropic Principle is that the same kind of argument can be used not just about planets, but about universes. Suppose that there are a huge number of universes. Some may have three space dimensions, some four, some five, and so one. In some the electromagnetic force may be weaker than the strong force, in others it may be stronger, and in others there may be no such thing as the electromagnetic force at all. And so on. That is, all sorts of possible physical laws are tried out in different universes. Then it would not be surprising, if enough universes existed, that some of them would have just the right laws of physics to allow life. And of course, to the inhabitants of such an exceptional universe, it might seem that someone was arranging things in their universe with then in mind.

Now before evaluating this idea, I should say that it comes in two very different versions. In one version, the different universes are really that: They are really utterly distinct and separate Universes. They have nothing to do with each other. They are not connected to each other in any way. They are, as it were, separate works. I will call this the "Many-Universe" idea. In the other version, the different so-called "universes" are really just different regions or "domains" or slices of one Universe. That is, there is really one Universe, and deep down all the parts of it are governed by one underlying set of physical laws. However, in different regions of that Universe, conditions may be so different as to make it seem – without a deep investigation – that the laws of physics are different. I will call this the "Many-Domain" idea.

Let me discuss these two idea separately.

(i) *The Many-Domain Hypothesis:*

The Many-Domain idea is not at all a foolish one. In fact, many of the kinds of theories that fundamental physicists think about nowadays naturally predict that there should be a domain structure to the universe. Far away from our galaxy – so far away, indeed, that it is beyond the "horizon" of physical observation – the universe may look very, very different. It may even look like it has a different number of dimensions. Moreover, it is very likely that some of the anthropic coincidences will be explained in the way envisioned in the Weak Anthropic Principle. However, I believe that it is intrinsically impossible to completely take away the force of the anthropic coincidences in this way. Why?

Well, what was the point of the anthropic coincidences in the first place. It was that the laws of physics have to be of a special kind to allow life to exist. But suppose we try to explain one of the anthropic coincidences – say that the world has three dimensions – by invoking the Many-Domain hypothesis. Then the laws of physics have to be such that they give rise to a domain structure and such, furthermore, that the number of space dimensions varies from domain to domain. That in itself requires that the laws of physics be very special! Moreover, it is not just one anthropic coincidence that has to be explained, but dozens and possibly hundreds of them. To explain them all by means of a Many-Domain scenario, one must assume that the laws of physics give rise to an enormously rich domain structure, in which a vast spectrum of possibilities is realized. That requires that the laws of physics be extremely special indeed! In other words, the Many-Domain hypothesis does not succeed in getting rid of the necessity of having very special laws of nature in order for life to be able to exist. One has simply traded specialness of one kind for specialness of another kind.

(ii) The Many-Universe idea.

The Many-Universe version does not suffer the same problem as the Many Domain version. In the Many-Domain idea, the laws of physics had to be engineered in such a way as to give rise a rich domain structure. In the Many-Universe idea, one just simply assumes that many types of Universes exist – by fiat. (Whose fiat? Don't ask!) The question must inevitably arise, then, which types of Universe exist and which types do not exist. That is not a question that the laws of physics can possibly answer. Each Universe has its own laws of physics. So if, say, Universes exist which have three space dimensions or four space dimensions, but no universes happen to exist which have seven space dimensions, that would seem to call for an explanation, but science itself cannot provide such an explanation. If some kinds of Universes exist while other kinds no not exist, then it would seem to suggest that Someone has made some choices. Far from getting away from the idea of a cosmic Designer, one is strengthening the case for it!

A last ditch way out for the opponents of cosmic design is to say that ALL possible Universes actually exist, i.e. any Universe that is logically and mathematically self-consistent actually exists. Out Universe exists just because it is logically self-consistent. This idea has a breathtaking simplicity. It would explain what existence is: existence would be the same as logical self-consistency. It would remove the need for a Designer. The "unique universe idea" got rid of a Designer by saying that there are an infinity of possibilities that could be selected among, but that no one has selected among them: they all exist!

There is a fatal problem with this way of getting rid of the cosmic Designer, however. It cannot explain why we live in a universe which is so astonishingly orderly and lawful. Among all the logically possible Universes, ones that have the perfection of order and lawfulness that ours has are highly exceptional, just as among all possible rocks, a perfect gem that has absolutely no flaws in it is almost infinitely unlikely. Why doesn't nature in our universe exhibit occasional departures from its regularities – the regularities we call the laws of physics – just as gemstones have occasional departures from their regularities? No answer to this is possible. In other words, if all possible universes exist, it becomes a tremendous miracle that we live in a universe of perfect, or nearly perfect lawlessness. It is a miracle, that is, the miracles do not occur around us all the time. The very lawfulness of nature becomes totally inexplicable.

Thus, the Weak Anthropic Principle, whether in its Many-Universe or Many-Domain forms, cannot succeed, in my view, in completely drawing the teeth of the anthropic coincidences. In the final analysis one cannot escape from two very basic facts: The laws of nature did not have to be as they are; and the laws of nature had to be of a very special form if life were to be able to exist. Between them these facts form the basis of a solid Design Argument for the existence of God.

FAITH AND BIOLOGICAL REDUCTIONISM: DARWIN AS A RELIGIOUS REFORMER

F. F. Centore

Multiply, vary, struggle to survive, let the strongest live and the weakest die. If you listen to the rhythm of the words it sounds like pleasant poetry. The content, though, is anything but pleasant. It's of dubious value in science, and it's certainly deadly in moral matters. Darwin, however, thought of himself as uttering the words of life, as teaching the gospel of the future. This gospel was the good news of biological reductionism. A long time before anyone heard of B.F. Skinner or E.O. Wilson there was Darwin. In fact, Darwin was such a reductionistic materialist that other thinkers, such as Marx and Dewey, because of their commitment to a non-reductionistic materialism, had to separate themselves from Darwin with respect to his philosophy of nature.

To understand why Darwin thought this way we must go back to the other big D in modern thought, the Frenchman Descartes. As most of us know from reading Gilson's *Unity of Philosophical Experience*, in more ways than one Descartes was not playing with a full deck of cards. Instead of 52 cards, his hand held only three. There was the God card, one and undivided, perfect in every way. Then came the mind card, made up of numerous souls, each separate from all the others, simple and undivided within themselves. Lastly there was the natural world card, created by God to be one and undivided in essence. Accordingly, the whole natural world is one thing, one being, with all differences being merely superficial variations. Is this something we observe? Not at all. It's the result of a deduction, not an induction.

It is in fact a matter of faith. We must trust the word of Descartes; we must believe in the existence of something we do not in fact see with our eyes. This unseen thing in which we must believe is pure extension, spread out in all three dimensions. This product of Descartes's imagination is nothing but continuous geometrical quantity. This one essence, out of which everything is made, leaves no room for truly different species. In contrast to Aquinas, who thought of species after the fashion of discrete quantities, such as the numbers in arithmetic, in Descartes's natural world all such divisions must be temporary and constantly subject to change. In such a world all natural types are as superficial as an A & E biography.[1]

---

[1] On species and numbers see Thomas Aquinas, *Summa Theologiae* I, 25, 6: "For the addition of a substantial difference in definitions is after the manner of the addition of unity in numbers." This, it seems, is the main problem. If each species is an incarnated idea, and if ideas don't change, then species cannot change. For an essentialist this poses an insurmountable barrier to species change. However, for a modern thomist, using Aquinas's own existential principles, it's possible to have species come into existence and go out of existence without denying God's providence. Unlike Plato, whose Ideas had an eternal independent existence, and Aristotle, whose Self-Thinking Thought couldn't and wouldn't create anything, He Who Is creates beings (essence and existence) freely selected from an infinite reserve of all possible beings, which is God himself. As a result, even though, once created, all members of a species are essentially the same, there is nothing preventing God from freely creating new species where and when he wills by whatever means he wills, including allowing for the operation of chance events. See *Summa Theologiae* I, 15, on the ideas, and 22, on providence. See also *Summa Theologiae* I, 45, 8; 67, 4, ad 3; 71; 74, 2; and Etienne Gilson, *Being and Some Philosophers* (Toronto: Pontifical Institute of Mediaeval Studies, 1952), pp. 182–83.

This is the scientific world into which Darwin (1809–1882) was born. Before Darwin such a view of nature had already been taken for granted by William Paley, who used it to prove that there must be an intelligent and good author of nature. Up to a point, Darwin was willing to go along with Paley. What Darwin didn't see, though, was the need for divine providence. Instead, Darwin thought in terms of deism, the doctrine that, although God may have originally created the world machine, he is now no longer exercising any direct and immediate care over it. In fact, what most likely happened is that God created the great world machine in some original state of imperfection and then left it to run on its own according to the fixed laws of nature inherent in it.

Originally there was only a huge amount of inanimate matter moving about in the endless reaches of space. Then perhaps God breathed life into a few things here and there. After that everything that we see today developed by a long series of accidents, changes that were not directed towards the production of anything in particular. It must have been through a series of accidents that *Homo sapiens* was regurgitated up out of the primeval slime, and then, by means of many trials and errors, later came up with notions about a spiritual life and the certitudes of physics and mathematics.

A rich source of information on the inner workings of Darwin's mind can be found in his letters, and also in his early notebooks, which were jotted down in the later 1830s. It's in the notebooks that we find the germinal ideas that were later elaborated upon in his main works. In this regard, it's interesting to discover that Darwin himself is by no means an anti-religious person. His family background was religious in nature. Indeed, throughout the greater part of his later life he made regular financial contributions to a Christian missionary society specializing in South America. What we find instead is an attempt on Darwin's part to alter the theology of Judaeo-Christianity in the direction of what he considered to be more scientific thinking. We can see this most clearly if we approach it from the viewpoint of the problem of evil.

On the basis of what he has to say in his early notebooks, letters, and public works, no one can doubt that Darwin takes the existence of evil seriously. Early in his career, while still more or less a believer in the Church of England religion of his beloved father, we find Darwin expressing the deepest regret over the way some human beings treat other human beings. Towards the end of his account of his work aboard H.M.S. Beagle, Darwin goes out of his way to add a section summarizing his moral revulsion at the institution of slavery. He notes how slaves are treated worse than dogs, and he thanks God that he is leaving Brazil, the last slave country on his trip.[2]

Imagine yourself in the degraded and hopeless condition of a lower class slave, says Darwin. In some rich household, perhaps, there might be such a thing as a happy slave, but certainly not in the countryside. Could you, he asks his middle class English readers, bear to be beaten, to have your families ripped away from you, and to be so humiliated that you are not capable of defending yourself when you are immediately and directly abused by an unjust owner? Can such things be done by people claiming to be Christians? Darwin concludes:

> It makes one's blood boil, yet heart tremble, to think that we Englishmen and our American descendants, with their boastful cry of liberty, have been and are so guilty.[3]

We find the same view expressed in his letters. Darwin writes to his confidant, the Harvard botanist Asa Gray (1810–1888), on 5 June 1861 that he is one of the few people in England who wish to God that the northern states would declare war on the southern states and start a crusade

[2] See Charles Darwin, *The Voyage of the Beagle*, L. Engel, ed. (Garden City, NY: Doubleday, 1962), p. 497.

[3] *Voyage*, p. 498.

against slavery. He says that even if a million deaths were to occur in such a crusade the beneficial effects to the rest of humanity would be well worth it. We live in wonderful times, he proclaims, because we may soon see the greatest curse on earth finally eliminated. Later, on 23 February 1863, he again writes to Gray, saying that he thinks it dreadful that the South, with its accursed slavery, might yet win the war.

Apparently, even after the publication of *The Origin of Species* (1859), Darwin still believes that some human acts are absolutely wrong. Earlier, in his B notebook (1837–1838), pages 231–232, he says that slave owners even go so far as to make blacks into an inferior species. Yet this is something he will not allow. If anything, we may want to go all the way in breaking down the barriers among species and claim that all creatures are brothers and sisters. If such a view were to have its full force, explains Darwin, not only would all humans be brothers, but all creatures would be netted together. This seems to imply that Darwin wants peace and harmony among all creatures.[4]

Yet, as we are told in all of his writings, the whole world is at war. In even the most peaceful looking, quiet, smiling fields there is constant warfare going on. Both early and late Darwin emphasizes this point. We find it in his E notebook (1838–1839), pages 63 and 114, as well as in a letter to William Graham of 3 July 1881. In the latter place he points out how the more civilized Caucasian race, because of its greater intellectual power, has triumphed over the Turks.

---

[4] All references to the notebooks are taken from H.E. Gruber and P.H. Barrett, *Darwin on Man* (New York: Dutton, 1974). References to Darwin's autobiography and letters are taken from F. Darwin, ed., *The Life and Letters of Charles Darwin: Including an Autobiographical Chapter*, 2 vols. (New York: Appleton, 1898 [first published in 1887]); F. Darwin, ed., *The Autobiography of Charles Darwin and Selected Letters* [1892] (New York: Dover, 1958); F. Darwin and A.C. Seward, eds., *More Letters of Charles Darwin: A Record of His Work in a Series of Hitherto Unpublished Letters*, 2 vols. (New York: Appleton, 1903).

And just think, he continues, of the countless number of less developed races that will surely be eliminated by the more advanced races. The result of such conflict, though, has to be something better, even for humans. In his B notebook, page 215, he states that mixing all the races together by interbreeding cuts down on the chances that a new and superior species will arise in the future. In his D notebook (1838–1839), pages 38–39, he observes that humankind is constantly changing, and that the Africans would very likely become a separate species in ten thousand years if there were no interbreeding with other races.

For Darwin there is no escaping the struggle for survival and hence no escaping evil. Evil is built right into the evolutionary process, both in terms of the imperfections of adaptation and of the animal heritage of human beings. The man who once thought about becoming a country clergyman asks about where we must look in order to find the source of our passions, passions that cause so much evil in the world. He thinks that they must be a carry-over from the past. Our descent, claims Darwin, is the source of our evil passions; the devil, in the form of a baboon, is our grandfather. Yet, in his M notebook (1838), pages 122–123, we find him saying to himself that the human passion of anger and the instinct for revenge must vanish, and indeed are vanishing, along with other vestiges of our animal past.

Over and over again we find the dean of Down House commenting on the existence of evil in the world. On 22 May 1860 he writes to Asa Gray that

> There seems to me too much misery in the world. I cannot persuade myself that a beneficent and omnipotent God would have designedly created the Ichneumonidae with the express intention of their feeding within the living bodies of caterpillars, or that a cat should play with mice.

Or what about the case, asks Darwin in a letter to Gray in July of the same year, of an innocent and good man, standing under a tree for protection, being struck down by lightning? Is this the way things should be?

Thinking about evil, he tells his cousin Julia Wedgwood in a letter dated 11 July 1861, puts his mind in a maze. Nevertheless, he's sure that evil could not have been purposefully designed into the universe by God. As he had told the Scottish geologist Charles Lyell (1797–1875) earlier, in a letter of April 1860, an omnipotent and omniscient God must control everything, and so must be responsible for evil as well as for good. Whether under human or divine guidance, it would still be a case of artificial selection. Is such a dual responsibility (good and evil) really what Lyell wants?

In a postscript to this letter, Darwin compares their quasi-theological debate over the merits of natural selection to the fully theological debates over predestination and the origin of evil. Ultimately, claims Darwin, all of these issues are beyond the power of the human intellect to solve. After all, the human intellect, as an aspect of the human body, also developed out of an ancient animal past. All we can do now is observe the fact of evil around us and try to account for it in general terms. We can be sure, though, that God is not responsible for it.

Somewhat later, the same point is made in a 14 December 1866 letter to Mrs. Boole. Presumably, this is Mary Boole, the wife of the mathematician George Boole (1815–1864), who, because he lived in the pre-computer era, was not as well-known in his own day as he is today. Mary, the daughter of a clergyman and the wife of a mathematician, had a long-standing interest in such matters. As Darwin explains, in answer to her question about the compatibility of faith and science, he is no expert on whether or not his doctrine is any more psychologically satisfying to the average believer than any other scientific doctrine. He then continues

> I may, however, remark that it has always appeared to me more satisfactory to look at the immense amount

> of pain and suffering in this world as the inevitable
> result of the natural sequence of events, i.e., general
> laws, rather than from the direct intervention of God,
> though I am aware this is not logical with reference to
> an omniscient Deity.

Judging by the end of his statement, Darwin seems to be aware of the fact that his position is not a true disjunction. As Darwin knew, numerous thinkers could find no contradiction between the existence of an all-knowing God and the existence of universal natural laws. Knowing that X will happen and wanting X to happen are not the same thing. Neither do universal natural laws indicate the need for deism. Furthermore, God's omniscience does not eliminate change and progress. The world, under divine guidance, could well be constantly changing for the better.

What Darwin seems to be telling Mrs. Boole is that, although it's theoretically possible to have both continuous divine providence and continuous species transmutation at the same time, he does not regard such a combination as fitting and proper. Being aware of the dominant natural theology of the day helps us understand his attitude. Following Descartes's mathematical approach to the world, God became the great engineer in the sky, the perfect mind, the majestic mathematician. Such a mind could only create the best of all possible worlds. For Darwin, any imperfection at all is incompatible with God the consummate engineer.

It seems, therefore, that Darwin does not reject divine providence because he's an atheist, but rather because he's still a religiously inclined thinker greatly troubled by evil as something real and objective. So, rather than blaming God for evil, it must instead be the case that the world is operating according to very strict laws that necessarily engender evil consequences. It's impersonal natural law that's responsible for evil, not the personal God of his beloved father. The dichotomy he's trying to get across to Mrs. Boole is the God of the old religion versus the God of the new religion, and that his new religion can preserve the best of the old religion while also being much more modern and scientific. No crackpot religion this. He can thus remain loyal to both his father and his science at the same time.[5]

As we might expect, Darwin's concern with evil also shows up in his main work. In the *Origin's* last chapter (15, Recapitulation and Conclusion) he emphasizes the fact that, according to his theory, it's only right and proper that there should be imperfection in the world. Why, he wonders, should the bee's use of its stinger kill it? Consider also all the wasted seeds and eggs, all the drone bees, produced only to be systematically slaughtered by their sterile sisters, and the way the queen bee systematically destroys her own fertile daughters. Consider how so many creatures destroy each other in order to survive, how some insects survive by eating their way through the living bodies of caterpillars, and how spiders use living captives to feed their own young.

Ironically, although he was never aware of what ailed him, it's now widely believed that Darwin's own heart, after he was bitten by an assassin bug while on the Beagle voyage, was infested with a flagellated protozoan parasite that takes up residence in the muscles of the heart. This dis-

[5] Darwin's mother, Susannah Wedgwood, known as Sukey, before she died in July of 1817, took little Charles to the Shrewsbury Unitarian Chapel. Following her death, Charles and his older sisters attended a day-school at the Chapel for a year. Charles, however, was baptized in the Church of England and attended Anglican services after 1818. He later (1827–1831) entered Christ's College in Cambridge, the same College attended by William Paley, with the intention of becoming a country clergyman. According to Darwin's son Francis, Darwin often said that his father was the wisest man he ever knew. And long after his father's death in 1848, at age 82, Charles could still remember in great detail his father's opinions on a wide variety of subjects. Further to Darwin's life see Adrian J. Desmond and James R. Moore, *Darwin* (London: Michael Joseph, 1991).

ease caused him to tire easily, and to stay home instead of frequently travelling to London for society and amusement. As we learn from the end of his autobiography, he regarded this as a blessing. It seems, therefore, that Darwin could agree with Aquinas that some evil things, at least, can be good. After all, says Thomas, if all evil were prevented much good would also be absent from the world.[6]

In the middle of chapter 15 Darwin's interest in moral issues is made quite clear. In this place he expresses himself on the significance of imperfection as part of a hierarchical series of points he's making on the value of natural selection relative to special creation. Among the things that could be easily explained by his view but that could not be explained very well by the old religion were the many strange anomalies in the world of living things, such as upland, land-bound geese having webbed feet. His view could also explain the great variation found among creatures with respect to what is and is not considered to be physically attractive. And finally, at the top of the hierarchy, comes the problem of evil. He states that

> Nor ought we to marvel if all the contrivances in nature be not, as far as we can judge, absolutely perfect, as in the case even of the human eye; or if some of them be abhorrent to our sense of fitness. . . . The wonder indeed is, on the theory of natural selection, that more cases of the want of absolute perfection have not been detected.

When things don't fit together properly there's conflict. Basically, evil is conflict, a maladjustment, a mismatch among things and the parts of things.

---

[6] On this point see *Summa Theologiae* I, 22, 2, ad 2. The disease that may have afflicted Darwin is called Chagas's Disease, named after the Brazilian doctor Carlos Chagas who discovered it in 1909. More recently it has been suggested that his ailment was more psychological than physical, namely, panic disorder. See "Darwin's Angst," Science 275 (24 January 1997), p. 487.

In his brief autobiography of 1876 Darwin tells us that early in life his constant companion on the Beagle voyage was John Milton's *Paradise Lost*, a work dealing with the battle between good and evil. And even towards the end of his life, in the Concluding Remarks to chapter 4 of the last edition of *The Descent of Man*, we are informed that the world is progressing every day towards higher and higher levels of morality, and that soon virtue will triumph. This is Darwin's *Ode to Joy*, his new religion's counterpart to Beethoven's Ninth Symphony.

For many years people have wondered why Darwin waited so long before publishing his theory. Indeed, if it had not been for the arrival on his doorstep of a very similar theory by Alfred Russel Wallace (1823–1913) he most likely would have waited even longer. However, if we take Darwin seriously as a religious thinker, the most likely explanation for his long delay was not the fear of persecution or respect for the traditional religious feelings of his family, but the desire to work out a new natural theology that could stand up to criticism by the representatives of the old religion. He didn't want his new-found faith subjected to the jeers of unbelievers. All historians today seem to be in agreement that Darwin's original intention was to publish a much longer work, loaded down with thousands of footnotes. So thank God for Wallace.

This attitude can be seen soon after his return from the Beagle voyage. In his C notebook (1838), page 75, we find Darwin struggling with the notion of great changes being explained by the accumulation of tiny changes. He complains that it's a laborious and painful effort. Nevertheless, despite its many problems, gradual transformationism is still more in keeping with all the waste and variation in the biosphere than is special creationism. Once let the persistent thinker apply himself to it, affirms Darwin, "then he will choose and firmly believe in his new faith of the lesser of the difficulties."

Darwin's reference to a new faith is significant. In the C notebook, page 174, we see that God and imperfect adaptation cannot coexist. Having wax in the ear is good for keeping out insects, but then why don't we have a body odor good at repelling insects, such as mosquitoes? It must be due to a lack of divine providence. The fitting together of the parts of nature are obviously imperfect; if the puzzle were perfectly constructed, no one animal would cause misery to any other animal.

Apparently intent upon not using anything taken from the old religion, such as Original Sin, Darwin asks if, from God's perspective, it's any harder to choose, by means of necessary, impersonal, mechanical laws of nature, at what point in history a semi-human, such as a Fuegian or an Australian Aborigine, will become fully human, than it is to decide who should go to heaven or hell? In Darwin's reductionistic view of reality, of course, there is no heaven or hell, but that's not the point. On page 244 of the C notebook Darwin wonders to himself why things should not proceed in fine gradations, thereby relieving God of the responsibility of making such momentous decisions, and also relieving God of the responsibility of having made so many bad ones.

There are other places in which Darwin gives away his hand as a religious reformer. He writes in a 26 September 1860 letter to Asa Gray that

> I yet hope and almost believe, that the time will come when you will go further, in believing a very large amount of modification in species, than you did at first or do now. Can you tell me whether you believe further or more firmly than you did at first?

Darwin then goes on to tell Gray that he is made confident in the future acceptance of his theory by the scientific community because of the converted attitudes of Charles Lyell and the English botanist Joseph Dalton Hooker (1817–1911). Darwin is happy to say that very soon after the publication of the *Origin* they had become believers.

This sort of language is not accidental on Darwin's part. He is an evangelist. He is out to make converts. The issue for him is much more than bloodless science. For years after the first publication of the *Origin* Darwin carefully scrutinized reviews of his work with one aim in mind, namely, to determine just how far the new leaders of the world, the scientists, were moving in the direction of his new religion.

An essential part of his new religion is the necessity of progress in the biosphere. Certainly, many species have become extinct in the past, and many more will go extinct in the future. But what of the overall picture? In contrast to those theologians who do not hesitate to read divine purpose into every detail of the biosphere, Darwin has no use for divine guidance in the details of animal structures. He does, however, firmly believe in an overall aim for natural selection. This commitment to a long-term teleology, howbeit without divine guidance, can be seen both early and late in Darwin's thinking.

On page 18 of his B notebook the mild-mannered rebel questions himself about the causes of change. He thinks that species can change, but do they progress? He wonders if there might not be a parallel between a human being gaining ideas and a species gaining traits. He then states that the simplest organisms must develop into something more complicated. Considering the overall history of the world, there must be progress. If we put his view in this place together with his views as stated on page 47 of his N notebook (1838–1839) and in an 11 January 1844 letter to Joseph Hooker, we see that, for Darwin, although there is no necessary tendency towards perfection with respect to individuals or particular species, there is with respect to the overall, long-term development of the biosphere. In this regard Darwin fits in very well with the spirit of the age, as can be seen in many others as well, such as Auguste Comte and Karl Marx. For Darwin, the perfection towards which nature is inexorably moving is the combination of the utmost in diversity, adaptation, and harmony among all the parts of the natural world.

Indeed, according to Dov Ospovat, as Darwin got older, and closer to writing the *Origin*, he became more convinced of progressivism, not less convinced. This is confirmed by what Darwin himself has to say in his major work. Necessary progress is affirmed by Darwin in the early part of chapter 7 (Miscellaneous Objections to the Theory of Natural Selection), at the very end of chapter 8 (Instinct), and in the second-last paragraph of chapter 15, near the end of the whole work.[7]

> Although we have no good evidence of the existence in organic beings of an innate tendency towards progressive development, yet this necessarily follows, as I have attempted to show in the fourth chapter, through the continued action of natural selection. For the best definition which has ever been given of a high standard of organization, is the degree to which the parts have been specialised or differentiated; and natural selection tends towards this end, inasmuch as the parts are thus enabled to perform their functions more efficiently.

[7] See Dov Ospovat, *The Development of Darwin's Theory: Natural History, Natural Theology, and Natural Selection, 1838–1859* (New York: Cambridge University Press, 1981). See in The Origin of Species and The Descent of Man (New York: Modern Library, [n.d.]), pp. 160, 208, 373. See also in the *Origin*, chapter 4 (Natural Selection; or The Survival of the Fittest), pp. 78, 98. I don't think that the importance of the problem of evil in Darwin's motivational psychology contradicts the presence of other important factors, such as the great biogeographical diversity of life forms, going into the construction of his theory. See Alan Richardson, "Biogeography and the Genesis of Darwin's Ideas on Transmutation," *Journal of the History of Biology* 14 (1981), pp. 1–41. On page 41 Richardson states: "His faith in, and strict adherence to, the doctrine of uniformitarianism played an essential role in his success." Without a time machine and without the possibility of repeating the events of the past in the present, Darwin, in order to justify extrapolating present conditions into the past, had to have faith in the fact that the geographical conditions of the world were the same throughout the entire history of biological development. Today, though, we know that worldwide catastrophes, as devastating as the biblical flood, have occurred in the past, some recently according to geological standards.

Finally, it may not be a logical deduction, but to my
imagination it is far more satisfactory to look at such
instincts as the young cuckoo ejecting its foster-broth-
ers – ants making slaves – the larvae of ichneu-
monidae feeding within the living bodies of caterpillars – not as specially endowed or created instincts,
but as small consequences of one general law leading
to the advancement of all organic beings, namely –
multiply, vary, let the strongest live and the weakest
die.

As all the living forms of life are the lineal descen-
dants of those which lived long before the Cambrian
epoch [600 million years ago], we may feel certain that
the ordinary succession by generation has never once
been broken, and that no cataclysm has destroyed the
whole world. Hence we may look with some confidence to a secure future of great length. And as natural selection works solely by and for the good of each
being, all corporeal and mental endowments will tend
to progress towards perfection.

In Darwin's thinking, the best of all possible world's is
slowly developing around us, but will not come into actual
existence until some time in the far distant future. In the
meantime the mixture of good and evil will remain with us.
In contrast to the doctrine of Original Sin, whereby evil is
not necessary, for Darwin evil is necessary; it's woven into
the very fabric of nature. Evil is a mismatch, a lack of coor-
dination, and is sure to be with us for a very long time. As
for human beings, they must learn to see themselves as
completely immersed in nature. They are accidents of evolution, regurgitated up out of the primeval slime. They
have nothing of which they can be excessively proud. Their
brains may be bigger than the rest, but, in terms of their
origin, they stand on a par with the rest of the biosphere.
Consequently, just as we should treat animals humanely, so
should we treat semi-human creatures with kindness and
compassion.

We must keep in mind that Darwin's whole emotional
outlook, inculcated into him by his family and society, was

to be morally good and conservative. Charles learned from his medical doctor father the value of being sensitive to moral issues, that it was generally a bad thing to cause people to despair, and that a good example is the best way to teach ethical behavior. Darwin felt deeply that, although he did not attempt to generalize factual knowledge under general laws (that is, to think scientifically), his father was the best man he ever knew. He learned early on that the moral aspect of life must not be overlooked.

What Darwin wanted was a combination of factors, an ideal synthesis that would preserve the best of the old ways of thinking while eliminating whatever is irrational. In other words, what the world needed was a new religion, and an able apologist to defend it. In this new religion there would still be a great deal of room for love and hope. There is still a well-founded hope for a far off event towards which the whole creation moves, but it would no longer be a pre-ordained divine event. In the darwinian faith, which was later adopted by so many process philosophers and theologians, it makes no sense to talk about the way things were planned in the beginning.[8]

As a religious reformer, therefore, Darwin was primarily interested in the problem of evil, and its ever-present twin, the problem of good. To Darwin, issues concerning whether or not natural selection is verifiable by repeatable experiments, the difference between direct and indirect creationism, the possibility of miracles, and whether or not natural selection is the only avenue for species change, are of secondary importance. The important thing is to keep the renovated, rational, scientific faith alive.

[8] Compare Alfred Tennyson (1809–1892), *In Memoriam A.H.H.*, the last stanza of the whole poem: "That God, which ever lives and loves, One God, one law, one element, And one far-off divine event, To which the whole creation moves." See also Philip G. Fothergill, *Historical Aspects of Organic Evolution* (London: Hollis and Carter, 1952), p. 121, on the way darwinianism was regarded in Germany as a new faith as early as 1877.

Today, though, at the end of the twentieth century, we have lived to see the actual consequences of Darwin's new religion. Even in his own day the signs of decay were visible to those with an eye to see them. According to Chesterton, when we look beneath the surface of Victorian life we see that

> Victorianism was not at all Victorian. It was a period of increasing strain. It was the very reverse of solid respectability; because its ethics and theology were wearing thin throughout.[9]

Darwinism is a good example of what Chesterton is talking about. Despite his good intentions, Darwin was naive in matters of history, philosophy, and theology. In an 11 August 1860 letter to Gray, for instance, apparently forgetting what he had said in the *Origin* about species being only convenient labels attached to groups of specimens, Darwin says that it's absurd for the Swiss-American naturalist and medical doctor Jean Louis Rodolphe Agassiz (1807–1873) to declare that, if species do not exist in the first place, then they cannot possibly change.

Darwin was just as naive in moral matters. For example, when in 1874 the English naturalist and physician St. George Jackson Mivart (1827–1900) publicly criticized Darwin's son George for advocating eugenics, Darwin became incensed, and told Mivart that he would never speak to him again. Darwin was apparently totally unaware of the negative social consequences of his own theory.[10]

In the same vein, A.O.J. Cockshut comments on the way Darwin's bulldog, Thomas Henry Huxley (1825–1895), at

---

[9] G.K. Chesterton, *Autobiography* (London: Hutchinson, 1937), p. 26.

[10] See Gertrude Himmelfarb, *Darwin and the Darwinian Revolution* (London: Chatto and Windus, 1959), pp. 57, 295–297. Mivart's *On the Genesis of Species* (New York: Appleton, 1871), is still worthwhile reading today.

the end of his career, asserted that in order to have a decent ethics we must now kick over the evolutionary ladder that got us here. Cockshut takes this as a clear admission of the perfect uselessness of darwinism as a guide in ethics. He observes that Huxley's words were the

> last articulate sound made by the old guard of English agnosticism, those strong, simple, immensely energetic, confident, moralistic men who never heard of Freud, and [who] ignored Marx and Kierkegaard and Nietzsche, the makers of the world we know [today in the twentieth century].[11]

Although it was articulated in the nineteenth century, the full consequences of Darwin's faith did not show up until the twentieth century, and they certainly were anything but peaceful and harmonious. Darwin's struggle for survival has been used to justify every sort of inhumanity imaginable, and is today only an embarrassment for the pragmatists, proportionalists, and postmoderns writing on ethics. Yes, it is possible to have faith in biological reductionism as a new religion, but, if you do, you must be prepared to abandon human freedom while embracing a moral relativism that would make even a monkey blush.[12]

---

[11] A.O.J. Cockshut, *The Unbelievers: English Agnostic Thought, 1840–1890* (New York: New York University Press, 1966), p. 178. See also the anthology edited by Cockshut, *Religious Controversies of the Nineteenth Century: Selected Documents* (Lincoln, NE: Nebraska University Press, 1966).

[12] See Albert Somit and Steven A. Peterson, *Darwinism, Dominance, and Democracy: The Biological Bases of Authoritarianism* (Westport, CT: Praeger, 1997), pp. 7–11, 101. According to these authors, in political terms religious nurture must overcome darwinian nature if democratic (one man, one vote) civilization is to survive and spread. More recently, the necessary relationship between biology and reductionism has been questioned within biology itself. See Nigel Williams, "Biologists Cut Reductionist Approach Down to Size," *Science* 277 (25 July 1997), pp. 476–77.

FAITH AND PROCREATION: THE FIGHT FOR THE FUTURE

Germain Kopaczynski, OFM Conv.

We live an age of sound bites.
"If it doesn't fit, you must acquit."
"Everybody lies about sex."
"Read my lips."
"If it feels good, do it."
"No new taxes."
"Just do it."
"The sex was consensual."
"Even presidents have private lives."
"Keep love and life together."

Whoa, Where did *that one* come from? It is the Church's sound bite regarding the proper use of human sexuality. It is the sound bite we shall be discussing in this presentation.

I want to thank the Fellowship of Catholic Scholars for affording me the opportunity to speak on this most important topic, "Faith and Procreation." I regard the aim of our Fellowship to be nothing less than helping its members and the entire Church appreciate Boethius' lapidary summation of Christian scholarship: "Join faith and reason, if you can."

In this presentation, the truth of *Humanae Vitae* is taken for granted.[1] How to impart this truth to the men and

---

[1] Paragraph 12 of *Humanae Vitae* is key: "This teaching, set forth by the Magisterium on numerous occasions, is founded upon the inseparable connection, willed by God and which man may not break on his own initiative, between the two-fold significance of the conjugal act: the unitive significance and the procre-

women of our day will be our prime concern.[2] We shall see
that the theme of faith and procreation involves us in a
fight for the future.

Humanae Vitae and The Past

With apologies to Whitehead, I would contend that the
safest general characterization of modern Western society

ative significance. Indeed, by its intimate structure, the conjugal
act, while closely uniting husband and wife, makes them apt for
the generation of new lives, according to laws inscribed in the
very being of man and woman. By safeguarding both these essential aspects, the unitive and the procreative, the conjugal act pre-
serves in its fullness the sense of true mutual love and its ordina-
tion to man's most high vocation to parenthood. We think that
men of our day are particularly capable of confirming the deeply
reasonable and human character of this fundamental principle."

[2] The following may be consulted with profit: United States
Catholic Conference, ed., *Crisis in Morality: The Vatican Speaks Out*
(Washington, DC: USCC, 1969); William E. May et al, eds.,
Principles of Catholic Moral Life (Chicago: Franciscan Herald Press,
1980); Ermenegildo Lio, O.F.M., *Humanae Vitae e conscienza:
Insegnamento di Karol Wojtyla teologo e Papa* (Vatican City: Libreria
editrice Vaticana, 1980); idem, *Humanae Vitae e infallibilita: Paolo
VI, il Concilio e Giovanni Paolo II* (Vatican City: Libreria Editrice
Vaticana, 1986); William E. May, *Contraception And Catholicism*
(Common Faith Tract No. 5) (Front Royal, VA: Christendom
Publications, 1983); Germain Grisez, Joseph Boyle, John Finnis
and William E. May, "Every Marital Act Ought to Be Open to
New Life: Toward a Clearer Understanding," *The Thomist* 52/3
(July 1988), pp. 365–426; Russell E. Smith, ed., *Trust the Truth: A
Symposium on Humanae Vitae* (Braintree, MA: Pope John Center,
1991); John Kippley, *Sex and the Marriage Covenant* (Cincinnati:
Couple to Couple League, 1991); Janet E. Smith, *Humanae Vitae: A
Generation Later* (Washington, D.C: The Catholic University of
America Press, 1991); Janet E. Smith, ed., *Why Humanae Vitae Was
Right: A Reader* (San Francisco: Ignatius Press, 1993); Kevin E.
Miller, "The Incompatibility of Contraception with Respect for
Life," *Life and Learning: Proceedings of the Seventh University Faculty
for Life Conference*, pp. 80–126.

is that it consists in a series of attempts to liberate itself from what it considers the oppressive yoke of the Judaeo-Christian ethical heritage, especially in the realm of sexual matters.

As the West continues on its course, one fact is becoming more and more clear: the more it distances itself from the Judaeo-Christian ethical tradition, the closer the West comes to a moral breakdown.[3] One reason for this stands out above all others: to speak of human sexuality in terms of liberation from moral standards rather than integration into the total human personality is, quite simply, to miss the entire point of what constitutes a civilization.[4] The Church knows this, an insight constituting a pivotal point to understand about the current situation.

Jesus Christ and His Dealings with Women

In a column appearing in the *Wall Street Journal* for August 13, 1993 entitled "The New Counterculture," Philip Lawler spoke approvingly of the outpouring of faith which greeted Pope John Paul II's visit to Denver for World Youth Day. The author went on to speak of Natural Family

---

[3] See for example Francis A. Schaeffer, *How Should We Then Live? The Rise And Decline Of Western Thought and Culture* (Westchester, IL: Crossway Books, 1976); James Hunter Davison, *Culture Wars: The Struggle to Define America* (New York: BasicBooks, 1991); William J. Bennett, *The De-Valuing of America: The Fight for Our Culture and Our Children* (New York: Summit Books, 1992); Stephen L. Carter, *The Culture of Disbelief: How American Law and Politics Trivialize Religious Devotion* (New York: BasicBooks, 1993); United States Catholic Bishops, *Confronting a Culture of Violence: A Catholic Framework for Action* (Washington, DC: USCC, 1994); Tom Sine, *Cease Fire: Searching for Sanity in America's Culture Wars* (Grand Rapids: Eerdmans, 1995).

[4] See the arguments made in Walter Lippmann, *A Preface To Morals* (New York: Macmillan, 1929); J.D. Unwin, *Sex And Culture* (Oxford: Oxford University Press, 1934); Pitirim A. Sorokin, *The American Sex Revolution* [An Extending Horizons Book] (Boston: Porter Sargent Publisher, 1956).

Planning as a moral method of exercising responsible parenthood. Lawler's article occasioned some negative letters to the editor. One – from a woman in Louisville, Kentucky – challenged him "to tell me why women world-wide should remain faithful to a male-dominated church that has for centuries feared the power of women and thus contrived to control them by casting them as madonnas or outcasting them as whores."[5]

The question she poses, why women remain faithful to the Church, should cause us to reflect. If human sexuality is an inappropriate area to speak of revolution, it seems to me that we *can* speak of an authentic *social revolution* in the way the founder of Christianity dealt with the women of his day.

In his dealings with the Samaritan woman and the woman taken in adultery and in the way he invited women to take part in his ministry, Jesus of Nazareth brought about a revolution whose effects are being felt to this day. Christ treated women in a way that must serve as the standard for any talk of authentic Christian feminism: men and women are equal in dignity, complementary in nature.[6] Almost all who call themselves "feminists" would agree with the first part of the sentence – "equal in dignity" – but many of them would fight tooth and nail against the second: "com-

[5] See the Letters to the Editor section in the *Wall Street Journal* (Sept. 1, 1993). Letter by Valerie Kane.

[6] Cf. Ann Brown, *Apology to Women: Christian Images of the Female Sex* (Leicester, UK: Inter-Varsity Press, 1991); Francis Martin, *The Feminist Question: Feminist Theology in the Light of Christian Tradition* (Grand Rapids: Eerdmans, 1994); Benedict Ashley, O.P., *Justice in the Church: Gender and Participation*, The McGivney Lectures of the John Paul II Institute for Studies on Marriage and the Family, 1992 (Washington, D.C: The Catholic University of America Press, 1996); Ecumenical Coalition of Women and Society, "Women of Renewal: A Statement," *First Things* 80 (1998), pp. 36–40; Angelo Scola, "The Dignity and Mission of Women: The Anthropological and Theological Foundations," *Communio* 25/1 (1998), pp. 42–56.

plementary in nature."[7] *Humanae Vitae* reminds the Church's sons and daughters that they must live both. "In his own image he created them, male and female he created them" (*Gen* 1:27). "And the Lord God saw that his creation was very good" (*Gen* 1:31). Indeed, *Humanae Vitae* is nothing less than a call for the Church to fight for the work of God.[8]

A Fight Against the Work of God

Herbert Marcuse once opined that the feminist revolution is in theory the most radical of all revolutions: the French and Russian revolutions were fought against the creations of human beings; the feminist revolution is a fight against the work of God.[9] I understand Marcuse to mean that feminism is a fight against that specific work of God

---

[7] Positive evaluation of complementarity is verboten in lock-step feminist discourse, and this holds for those who regards themselves as 'religious' feminists as well. Madonna Kolbenschlag, *Kiss Sleeping Beauty Good-Bye: Breaking the Spell of Feminine Myths and Models* (New York: Bantam New Age Books, 1981), p. 113, views complementarity as "a disguised neurotic symbiosis that perpetuates immaturity." See also the comments made by Catherine Mowry LaCugna, "Catholic Women as Ministers and Theologians," *America* 167/10 (October 10, 1992), pp. 238–248, and those of Sister Marie Vianney Bilgrien, "The Voice of Women in Moral Theology," *America*, 173/20 (December 16–23, 1995), pp. 13–20.

[8] I have written on this in "A Fight for the Work of God," *Homiletic and Pastoral Review*, 95/10 (1995), pp. 23–32.

[9] Herbert Marcuse, "Marxismus und Feminismus," *Jahrbuch für Politik* 6 (1974), p. 86, speaks of feminism as "possibly the most important and potentially radical movement of contemporary life." It is quoted in Jutta Burggraf, "The Mother of the Church and the Woman in the Church in the Church: a Correction of Feminist Theology Gone Astray," in Helmut Moll, ed., *The Church and Women: a Compendium* (San Francisco: Ignatius Press, 1988), p. 239 note 7. Cf. Mary O'Brien, *The Politics of Reproduction* (Boston: Routledge and Kegan Paul, 1981), p. 26: "Feminism has redefined revolution." Cf. Danielle Lafontaine, "Profondeur historique et

that is the human person made in God's image as male and female.[10]

If in one sense *Humanae Vitae* served as a commentary upon Vatican II's *Gaudium et Spes*, we do well to remind ourselves that the question of atheism was one of the major concerns of the Second Vatican Council.[11] The question of the human being is unanswerable in Christian context without reference to the God who creates:

> "For the Church holds that the recognition of God is
> in no way hostile to man's dignity, since this dignity is

dimension politique de la cause des femmes," *Cahiers de recherche éthique* 8 (1981): "Devenirs de femmes," pp. 21–38, especially p. 27. We should, of course, be wary of failing to distinguish between the various feminisms. There are secular and religious feminisms, for one, proabortion and prolife feminisms for another.

[10] Note how John T. Noonan, Jr., *Abortion in Our Culture* (Washington, D.C: National Conference of Catholic Bishops' Committee for Pro-Life Activities, 1980), p. 5, explains the rise of the current abortion mentality: "These profound cultural drives toward absolute freedom and absolute control are comprehensible as expressions of an underlying atheism. If God does not exist, there are no limits – moral, social, or even biological. If God does not exist, it is each individual for himself or herself. If God does not exist, human control must replace divine providence. This underlying atheism is rarely articulated. Even many religious persons share the modern desires, breathing them in from the surrounding atmosphere, without attending to the atheism which is their source. But when human beings in the name of human liberty assert the power to destroy innocent human life, it is plain that they have put themselves in the place of God as the Lord and Giver of Life. Abortion is atheism put into practice." For the link between abortion and atheism, see also F. LaGard Smith, *When Choice Becomes God* (Eugene, OR: Harvest House Publishers, 1990); Damian P. Fedoryka, *Abortion and the Ransom of the Sacred* (Front Royal, VA: Christendom Press, 1991); and my *No Higher Court: Contemporarary Feminism and the Right to Abortion* (Scranton, PA: University of Scranton Press, 1995.)

[11] Cf. Gaudium et Spes, paragraphs 19 through 21.

rooted and perfected in God. *For man was made an intelligent and free member of society by the God who created him.*" [*Gaudium et Spes*, 21; my emphasis].

Humanae Vitae is a commentary upon this insight made in *Gaudium et Spes*. God created human beings intelligent; God created human beings free. But it is of utmost importance for an authentic Christian anthropology to remember that it is God who creates human beings.

I have my own sound bite for the essence of Christian anthropology: "God is Lord of Life and Death, we the in-between." In the work that goes on at The National Catholic Bioethics Center, perhaps 40% of our consultations deal with questions regarding life at the very beginning, while another 40% deal with life at the very end.[12] Indeed, we at the Center find ourselves referring over and over again to two sections of the 1994 statement of the National Conference of Catholic Bishops, the *Ethical and Religious*

---

[12] The theme of "life at the edges" is treated in Paul Ramsey's book , *Ethics at the Edges of Life: Medical and Legal Intersections* (New Haven: Yale University Press, 1978). It is also featured in Pope John Paul II's *The Gospel of Life*. According to Karl Barth, "No community whether family, village or state is really strong if it will not carry its weak and even its very weakest members. They belong to it no less than the strong, and the quiet work of their mainteneance and care, which might seem useless on a superficial view, is perhaps more effective than common labor, culture or historical conflict in knitting it closely and securely together. On the other hand, a commuity which regards and treats its weak members as a hindrance, and even proceeds to their expermination, is on the verge of collapse." Barth's text from Church Dogmatics (1961) is cited in Kenneth L Garver and Bettylee Garver, "Eugenics, Euthanasia, and Genocide," *The Linacre Quarterly* 59/3 (August 1992), p. 46. The late American politician Hubert Humphrey put it this way: "The moral test of government is how it treats those who are in the dawn of life, the children; those who are in the twilight of life, the aged; and those who are in the shadows of life, the sick, the needy, the handicapped."

Directives for Catholic Health Care Services, namely, Part Four, "Issues in Care for the Beginning of Life," and Part Five, "Issues in Care for the Dying." It is precisely here that the rubber hits the road regarding life and death, human responsibility and God's prerogatives. Are we responsible stewards or absolute masters?[13]

To defend the prerogatives of God is to uphold the dignity of the man and the woman made in His image and likeness. Indeed, that this is the case we see in the importance John Paul II gives to this passage from paragraph 24 of *Gaudium et Spes*:

> "This likeness reveals that man, who is the only creature on earth which God willed for itself, cannot fully find himself except through a sincere gift of himself."[14]

In Christian marriage, the spouses participate in the creative action of God. When Pope John Paul II deals with the subject of intrinsically disordered actions in *Veritatis*

[13] For more on this, see the article by James Keating, Ph.D. and John Corbett, O.P., "Euthanasia and the Gift of Life," *The Linacre Quarterly* 63 (August 1996), pp. 33–41, who are discussing an argument being advanced by Dick Westley, *When It's Right to Die: Conflicting Voices*, Difficult Choices (Mystic, CT: Twenty-Third Publications, 1995). Along the same lines, see Russell Hittinger, "Law and Liberty in 'Veritatis Splendor'," in *The Splendor of Truth and Health Care*, (Braintree: The Pope John Center, 1995), pp.29–42, and my "Stewardship, Dominion and Autonomy" [Part 21 of the Series: Catholic Tradition and Bioethics], *Ethics & Medics*, 20/9 (1995), pp. 1–2.

[14] John Paul II uses paragraph 24 of *Gaudium et Spes* in *The Splendor of Truth*, 13 and 86, and in *The Gospel of Life*, 96. The thought behind the paragraph is a staple in his addresses as well. See for example his "Message to the Pontifical Academy of Sciences on Evolution," *Origins* 26/22 (November 14, 1996), pp. 350–52.

Splendor, his reasoning shows that the faithfulness of the Church involves her sons and daughters in a fight for the work of God in human affairs.[15]

Humanae Vitae and the Question of Woman

"One is not born, but rather becomes, a woman." All of contemporary feminism is a commentary on this one sentence of Simone de Beauvoir.[16] This statement lies at the heart of contemporary feminism.

[15] We read in paragraph 80 of *Veritatis Splendor*: "Reason attests that there are objects of the human act which are by their nature 'incapable of being ordered' to God, because they radically contradict the good of the human person made in his image."

[16] Simone de Beauvoir, *The Second Sex*, trans. and edited by H.M. Parshley (New York: Bantam Books, 1962), p. 249. This is a one-volume English abridgement of Beauvoir's two-volume *Le deuxième sexe* (Paris: Gallimard, 1949). Beauvoir's culturalist thesis is featured prominently in Sherry B. Ortner, "Is Female to Male as Nature is to Culture?" in Michelle Zimbalist Rosaldo and Louise Lamphere, eds., *Woman,Culture, and Society* (Stanford: Stanford University Press, 1974), pp. 67–87; it is reprinted in Marilyn Pearsall, ed., *Women and Values: Readings in Recent Feminist Philosophy* (Belmont, CA: Wadsworth, 1986), pp. 62–75. Elisabeth Badinter carries on this legacy of Beauvoir's culturalism in two works: *L'amour en plus: histoire de l'amour maternel: XVIIe–XXe siècle* (Paris: Flammarion, 1980), and *L'un est l'autre: des relations entre hommes et femmes* (Paris: Éditions Odile Jacob, 1986). Among the authors who note the importance of this text – "one is not born, but rather becomes, a woman"– as a key to reading not only Beauvoir but also contemporary feminism are Ruth Bleier, *Science and Gender: A Critique of Biology and Its Theories on Women*, The Athene Series (New York: Pergamon Press, 1984); Ginette Castro, *American Feminism: a Contemporary History*, trans. E. Loverde-Bagwell, Feminist Crosscurrents Series (New York: New York University Press, 1990); Jacques Ehrmann, "Simone de Beauvoir and the Related Destinies of Woman and Intellectual," *Yale French Studies* 27 (1961), pp. 26–32; Sara Ruddick, *Maternal Thinking: Toward a Politics of Peace* (New York: Ballantine Books, 1989); Beatrice Slama, "Simone de Beauvoir: Feminine Sexuality

In paragraphs 2 and 17 of *Humanae Vitae*, we find Pope Paul VI speaking of the role of women in the 20th-century. He makes reference, in paragraph 2, to the fact that there have been changes in how society has come to view woman. In paragraph 17, the impact artificial methods of birth control will have on the psyche of women and how men will come to view women form the basis for the second of Paul VI's four sadly-accurate prophecies regarding the fruits of a contraceptive mentality.[17] As Archbishop Chaput has recently observed, Pope Paul VI was right about the consequences of contraception because he was right about the evil of contraception itself.[18]

As woman goes, so goes the Church; as woman goes, so goes the world. Such seems to be the thought of Pope Paul VI in paragraphs 2 and 17 of *Humanae Vitae*. The fight over

and Liberation," in Elaine Marks, ed., *Critical Essays on Simone de Beauvoir*, pp. 218–234; Evélyne Sullerot, ed., *Le fait féminin*, Préface de Andre Lwoff (Paris: Fayard, 1978); Odette Thibault, *Débout les femmes*, Collection: L'Essentiel (Lyon: Chronique sociale, 1980); Anne Whitmarsh, *Simone de Beauvoir and the Limits of Commitment* (Cambridge: Cambridge University Press, 1981). Cf. Piersandro Vanzan, S.I., "Il femminismo contemporaneo: crisi, rilancio e prospettive," La Civiltà Cattolica 134, v. II, no. 3187 (7 maggio 1983), p. 263. He regards this text – "On ne naît pas femme: on le devient" – as the key culturalist text of contemporary feminism, an observation made a quarter of a century earlier by Lucius F. Cervantes, S. J., *And God Made Man and Woman: a Factual Discussion of Sex Differences* (Chicago: Regnery, 1959).

[17] The four prophecies embedded in *Humanae Vitae* 17: 1. There will be a lowering of morality coupled with increasing conjugal infidelity; 2. Men will tend to lose respect for the woman both physically and psychically; 3. The state will be tempted to interfere with conjugal morality; and 4. Individuals will buy into the illusion of absolute bodily autonomy.

[18] Archbishop Charles Chaput, "The Truth and Meaning of Married Love," *Origins* 28/14 (September 17, 1998), pp. 248–51, where the Archbishop's pastoral letter of July 22, 1998 is entitled "A Misunderstood Papal Intervention."

Humanae Vitae has been and continues to be not only a fight for the work of God but also a fight for the future of the feminine.

A Personal Experience

The setting was Northampton, Massachusetts, home of Smith College, alma mater of Gloria Steinem. The time was twenty years after the issuance of *Humanae Vitae*. Father Owen Bennett, my philosophy professor and long-time friend, and I approached the little group of approximately 25 young ladies. They were sitting on the ground in a semi-circle and chanting the refrain: "Our bodies, our lives, our right to decide."

They were protesting the fact that a pro-life lecture was about to be delivered on the campus of Smith College by Alice von Hildebrand who was speaking on the topic "Feminism, Abortion, and Motherhood." On the ride back home, we discussed the two messages we had heard that night, pro-abortion outside the hall, pro-life within. It occurred to me that the chant outside the hall and the lecture within were also part of that same commentary upon the one sentence from Simone de Beauvoir. While Von Hildebrand's words were most persuasive to those who heard them: "Abortion is an affront to women," the words of the mantra – "Our bodies, our lives, our right to decide" – were strong enough to keep the chanters from hearing the message within.

When I teach, I find myself using my own mantra, sound bite if you will: "*Fight For Words.*" Don't let words slip by unnoticed and unweighed. Is it possible to attach too much weight to words? Judging by the weighing of words going on in Washington these days, I hardly think so. In this I find myself in good company. Here again is the mother of modern feminism:

> "By trade, by vocation, I attach an enormous importance to words. Simone Weil used to demand that any-

one who used writing to tell lies to men should be put on trial, and I understand what she means. There are words as murderous as gas chambers."[19]

The Male as Model

In the process leading to her confirmation as a Supreme Court Justice, the then-nominee Ruth Bader Ginsburg said:

> "It is essential to a woman's equality with man that she be the decision-maker, that her choice be controlling. If you impose restraints, you are disadvantaging her because of her sex. The state controlling a woman would mean denying her full autonomy and full equality."[20]

Ginsburg's reasoning enshrines at the heart of much of contemporary feminist thought the victory of "The Male as Model" theory. Ginsburg's expression, "Full autonomy and

[19] Simone de Beauvoir, *Force of Circumstance*, trans. R. Howard (London: André Deutsch and Weidenfeld and Nicolson, 1965), pp. 21–22. Anyone acquainted with the abortion debate knows how deadly accurate Beauvoir's observation can be. Some words – "choice" for one – can kill. Notes Bill Bolte: "Choice is becoming a code word for the powerful eliminating the powerless." Bolte's words come from the article, "Be Wary Of These 'Last Rights,'" *USA Today* (February 24, 1993), p. 13A. Explaining why feminists like herself can still approve of President Clinton despite the Lewinsky affair, Wendy Kaminer, "Why Women Can Still Support This Man," *The Boston Sunday Globe* (September 20, 1998), p. F1, puts in first place "preserving and expanding reproductive choice."

[20] Neil A. Lewis, "Ginsburg Embraces Right of a Woman to Have Abortion," *The New York Times* (Thursday, July 22, 1993). The thought, of course, is not original with Ginsburg. Cf. Susan Moller Okin, *Women in Western Political Thought* (Princeton, NJ: Princeton, 1979), p. 301: "Women cannot become equal citizens, workers or human beings – let alone philosopher-queens – until the functionalist perception of their sex is dead."

full equality," has become a code expression for the theory
that holds that women are at a disadvantage in their dealings with the world of men as long as they bear the young
of the species. Irish novelist Edna O'Brien has a character in
one of her novels say: "Oh God who does not exist, you
hate women, otherwise you'd have made them different."[21]
Here the "Male as Model Theory" flows into the radical
feminist plaint that "Nature Is Misogynist."[22]

Radical secular feminists are not alone in espousing
some version of this theory. Here, for example, is a past
President of the Catholic Theological Society of America:

---

[21] Edna O'Brien, *The Country Girls Trilogy and Epilogue* (New
York: Farrar, Straus, Giroux, 1986), p. 473. I believe these words
are uttered by a male obstetrician. In one sentence we find the
question of God, atheism, a misogynistic nature, the abortion
issue, and the Male as Model Theory all rolled up into one neat
feminist package.

[22] Canadian feminist Shulamith Firestone's *The Dialectic of
Sex: The Case for Feminist Revolution* (New York: Bantam, 1970) is
the most extreme example of this approach. In her work, Marx
meets cybernetic socialism. Her critics are legion. Cf. Carol
McMillan, *Women, Reason and Nature: Some Philosophical Problems
With Feminism* (Princeton, NJ: Princeton University Press, 1982),
pp. 115ff. She argues that Firestone is saying, in effect, that it is
nature rather than *patriarchy* that is the great oppressor of women.
As McMillan sees it, "the women's liberation movement is a
rebellion against nature" (p. 118). Christine Delphy, *Close to Home:
a Materialist Analysis of Women's Oppression*, trans. and edited D.
Leonard (Amherst: University of Massachusetts Press, 1984), p.
143, contends that Firestone's thesis is "outrageously biologistic."
To feminists attached to a *culturalist* interpretation, the Firestone
thesis, especially regarding nature, is anathema. Hence, the comment made by Lisa Tuttle, *Encyclopedia of Feminism*, s. v. "The
Dialectic of Sex" p. 83: "The book's conclusions alienated many
feminists who are unwilling to locate the cause of women's
oppression in anything inherent in women: and there is also an
unwillingness to rely on technology – for so long used by men
against women – to provide the means of liberation."

"Full interpersonal and sexual reciprocity of women and men implies equality in all spheres of familial and social life. . . . Full equality in family, church, and society likewise implies the necessity to control reproduction adequately to permit women as well as men to mesh family life with their contributions in other spheres."[23]

Remember: we must fight for words so the phrasing is important: "Full equality implies . . . the control of reproduction." How is this to be understood? Does this control of reproduction imply Gloria Steinem's concept of "reproductive freedom" of birth control with abortion as backup?[24] If it does, we would do well to keep in mind that it is

[23] Lisa Sowle Cahill, "Catholic Sexual Ethics and the Dignity of the Person: A Double Message," *Theological Studies* 50 (March 1989), pp. 120–150; quote is from p. 146. Cahill may well be borrowing the expression from Rosemary Radford Reuther, *Sexism and God-Talk* (Boston: Beacon Press, 1983), pp. 18–19; there the code expression is "full humanity." It may be worth noting that while Cahill and others speak of "reproduction," the theme of this Convention address is "procreation."

[24] Cf. the entry "Reproductive Freedom" in Cheris Kramarae and Paula A. Treichler, *A Feminist Dictionary* (London: Pandora, 1985; rpt. 1989), p. 391. Steinem takes pride in having coined the expression, "Reproductive Freedom." See Nancy McGlen and Karen O'Connor, *Women's Rights: The Struggle for Equality in the Nineteenth and Twentieth Centuries* (New York: Praeger, 1983). Australian feminist Germaine Greer looks with favor on the use of abortion as a birth control backup in her *Sex and Destiny: the Politics of Human Fertility* (New York: Harper and Row, 1984), p. 231: "Abortion is an extension of contraceptive technology, and the most promising extension of it at that." Peter Riga, "The Splendor of Truth (*Veritatis Splendor*)," *The Linacre Quarterly* 63 (1995), pp. 26–32, has observed that for Justice Anthony Kennedy, abortion as backup to contraception has become part of the very fabric of our society. We read in *Planned Parenthood v. Casey*: "For two decades of economic and social developments, people have organized intimate relationships and made choices that define their views of themselves and their places in society, in reliance on

the same Gloria Steinem who has written: "By the year 2000 we will, I hope, raise our children to believe in human potential, not God."[25]

In fighting for words, we quickly discover that we are involved in fighting for the work of God. The fact that human beings are males and females: is this something to be fought and corrected by technological means or something to be embraced as the design of a loving God? A one-time dissenter from *Humanae Vitae* who has since become a defender of the truth of the encyclical, Jesuit Richard Roach, when speaking of the unequal roles that men and women play in the drama of procreation, has observed: "This is either a dispensation of profound spiritual significance or it is the damnedest injustice in creation."[26]

the availability of abortion in the event that contraception should fail. The ability of women to participate equally in the economic and social life of the Nation has been facilitated by their ability to control their reproductive lives." The text of *Casey* may be found in *Origins* 22/ 8 (July 9, 1992), pp. 113–56. The quote in question is found on page 118. Justice Kennedy was joined in the opinion by Justices O'Connor and Souter.

[25] The text of Steinem is found in Maggie Tripp, ed., *Woman in the Year 2000* (New York: Arbor House, 1974), p. 50.

[26] Richard Roach, S. J., "Moral Theology and the Mission of the Church: Idolatry in Our Day," in William E. May, ed., *Principles of Catholic Moral Life* (Chicago: Franciscan Herald Press, 1980), p. 35. Others pose the question in different ways: "I asked a friend, mother of six children, with a family income of £18 per week whether she thought financial or sexual inequalities were the greatest. After some thought, she said that *being a woman was the most unequal thing.*" Text found in Juliet Mitchell, *Woman's Estate* (New York: Vintage Books, 1973), p. 178, note 1: my emphasis. For more on this theme, see my article, "Is Nature Misogynist?," *Homiletic and Pastoral Review*, 95/4 (1995), pp. 22–30. See also Jean Bethke Elshtain, *Power Trips and Other Journeys: Essays in Feminism as Civic Discourse* (Madison: University of Wisconsin Press, 1990), pp. 110–15; Donald DeMarco, *Biotechnology and the Assault on Parenthood* (San Francisco: Ignatius Press, 1991), p. 251. The list is by no means

"Faith and Procreation"– The entire theme of our presentation today is wrapped up in this either/or just presented: if the complementarity of the sexes is the design of a loving God, what the Church teaches in *Humanae Vitae* and *Donum Vitae* makes perfect sense; if, on the other hand, we can reconstruct ourselves by means of pills and potions, prophylactics and surgical procedures, to be interchangeable, as it were, the gift of self – that total self-giving which is the heart of *Gaudium et Spes* 24 – is stripped of its meaning. Technology trumps truth.[27]

Perhaps we can boil down the issue of faith and procreation in this manner: Why must we keep the life-giving and the love-giving meanings of conjugal union together when technology can separate them? Here we have in a nutshell the challenge of teaching and living *Humanae Vitae*. And *Donum Vitae* as well. Together the two documents frame the parameters of our discourse on faith and procreation. At issue here is the question of the technological impera-

---

exhaustive. Some pertinent remarks on the general topic of sex differences in general and their relevance to ethical decision-making are made by William T. Blackstone, "Freedom and Women," *Ethics* 85/3 (1975), pp. 243–248. Similar thoughts are voiced by Ingrid Bengis, *Combat in the Erogenous Zones* (New York: Alfred A. Knopf, 1972), esp. p. 82.

[27] It is hard to overstate the importance of the *human* element when talking about authentic human sexual expression. We see it in paragraph 193 of Pope John XXIII's 1961 encyclical, *Mater et Magistra*: "In this connection, we strongly affirm that human life is transmitted and propagated through the instrumentality of the family which rests on marriage, one and indissoluble, and, so far as Christians are concerned, elevated to the dignity of a sacrament. Because the life of man is passed on to other men deliberately and knowingly, it therefore follows that this should he done in accord with the most sacred, permanent, inviolate prescriptions of God. Everyone without exception is bound to recognize and observe these laws. Wherefore, in this matter, *no one is permitted to use methods and procedures which may indeed be permissible to check the life of plants and animals* [my emphasis]."

tive: if we can do something, then we ought to do it. Technological prowess dictates morality. Or does it?[28]

If so, such an approach is in its essence a flight from the work of God that is the masculine and the feminine, and it becomes an embrace of "The Male as Model Theory."[29] It is only when women can pattern themselves on the male model of sex without consequences – men do not become pregnant, after all – that full equality and full humanity can come about.[30] When Ginsburg says what she does about

[28] Pope John Paul II has been warning of the dangers of the technological imperative throughout his pontificate. He is not alone. The National Conference of Catholic Bishops, *Ethical and Religious Directives for Catholic Health Care Services*, in the Introduction to Part Four, "Issues at the Beginning of Life," puts the matter this way: "With the advance of the biological and medical sciences, society has at its disposal new technologies for responding to the problem of infertility. While we rejoice in the potential for good inherent in many of these technologies, *we cannot assume that what is technically possible is always morally right*" [my emphasis]. Along the same lines, see Stanley Hauerwas, *Dispatches from the Front: Theological Engagements with the Secular* (Durham, NC: Duke University Press, 1994). A major proponent of the technological imperative is John Harris, *The Value of Life: An Introduction to Medical Ethics* (London: Routledge and Kegan Paul, 1985), and *Wonderwoman and Superman: The Ethics of Human Biotechnology*, Studies in Bioethics Series (New York: Oxford University Press, 1992).

[29] Note how Pope John Paul II speaks of the issue in paragraph 99 of *The Gospel of Life*: "In transforming culture so that it supports life, women occupy a place in thought and action which is unique and decisive. It depends on them to promote a 'new feminism' which rejects the temptation of imitating models of "male domination" in order to acknowledge and affirm the true genius of women in every aspect of the life of society and overcome all discrimination, violence and exploitation." The Male as Model Theory is a leitmotif in my *No Higher Court: Contemporary Feminism and the Right to Abortion*.

[30] Without belaboring the point, there is a sense in which men do become pregnant, an observation made by feminist soci-

"full autonomy and full equality," the *appearance* is that this is feminism, the *reality* is that here we have male values masquerading in feminist language.[31]

Whatever else an authentic Christian feminism might be, it too will have to fight for the work of God that is woman as she is and not the cultural construct of Beauvoir and Ginsburg.[32] An authentic Christian feminism will strive to safeguard the moral right of women to full social equality.[33] Women will do this, not by patterning

ologist Kristin Luker, *Taking Chances: Abortion and the Decision Not to Contracept* (Berkeley: University of California Press, 1975), p. 136.

[31] Laurence Tribe, *Abortion: The Clash of Absolutes* (New York: Norton, 1991), p. 132, puts it this way: "A ban on abortion imposes truly burdensome duties only on women. Such a ban thus places women, by accident of their biology, in a permanently and irrevocably subordinate position to men." As Guido Calabresi, *Ideals, Beliefs, Attitudes and the Law: Private Law Perspectives on a Public Law Problem* (New York: Syracuse University Press, 1985), p. 101, views the issue: "Without a right to abortion women are not equal to men in the law. They are not equal to men with respect to unburdened access to sex – with respect, that is, to sexual freedom." Is what we have in Tribe and Calabresi a reincarnation of sorts of Aristotle's view of the woman as misbegotten male? Just asking.

[32] Can there be an authentic Christian feminism? We have already seen that the author of *The Gospel of Life*, no. 99, seems to answer 'yes' to the question. See also Denise Lardner Carmody, *Virtuous Woman: Reflections on Christian Feminist Ethics* (Maryknoll: Orbis Books, 1992); Mary Ann Glendon, "The Pope's New Feminism," *Crisis* (March 1997), pp. 28–31.

[33] We have noted earlier that the fight for the work of God will involve us in the fight for the future of the feminine. Must this entail a return to the "eternal feminine"? Some works on the subject are worth investigating: Gertrud von LeFort, *The Eternal Woman: The Woman In Time, Timeless Woman*, trans. with a Preface by Placid Jordan, O.S.B. (Milwaukee: Bruce Publishing Co., 1962); Karl Stern, *The Flight From Woman* (New York: Noonday Press, 1965). Also helpful are Jean Guitton, *Feminine Fulfillment*, trans.

themselves on a male model but by respecting their own female sexuality. New Zealander Daphne De Jong puts it this way:

> "To say that in order to be equal with men it must be possible for a pregnant woman to become unpregnant at will is to say that being a woman precludes her from being a fully functioning person. . . . Of all the things which are done to women to fit them into a society dominated by men, abortion is the most violent invasion of their physical and psychic integrity."[34]

Humanae Vitae and the Present

To help us understand the present situation I would like to employ two acronyms. As the last decade of the 20th century winds down, two principles spoken of by Freud and embodying two differing worldviews of human sexuality are in conflict: The Pleasure Principle and the Reality Principle.[35] P.l.e.a.s.u.r.e. stands for the Practically Limitless Expression of Any Sexual Urge is a Right of Everyone.

Paul J. Oligny, O.F.M with Preface by Fulton J. Sheen (Chicago: Franciscan Herald Press, 1965); Louis Bouyer, *Woman in the Church*, trans. Marilyn Teichert (San Francisco: Ignatius Press, 1979).

[34] Daphne de Jong, "The Feminist Sell–Out," *New Zealand Listener* (January 14, 1976). It is reprinted with the title, "Legal Abortion Exploits Women," in Charles P. Cozic and Stacey L. Tipp, eds., *Abortion: Opposing Viewpoints*, Opposing Viewpoints Series (San Diego: Greenhaven Press, 1991), pp. 183–86. DeJong's comment makes its way into Maggie Gallagher, *Enemies of Eros: How the Sexual Revolution Is Killing Family, Marriage, and Sex and What Can We Do About It* (Chicago: Bonus Books, 1989), p. 233. In his recent letter on the truth of Pope Paul VI's encyclical, Archbishop Chaput observed: "Many feminists have attacked the Catholic Church for her alleged disregard of women, but the church in *Humanae Vitae* identified and rejected sexual exploitation of women years before that message entered the cultural mainstream."

[35] For more on Freud's use of the two principles, see Guido

R.e.a.l.i.t.y. stands for the Reliable Experience of Amative Lifegiving Is Truth's Yardstick.

We glimpse the Pleasure Principle in Simone de Beauvoir's *The Second Sex*. We see it fully developed in a 1976 statement of the American Humanist Association: "A New Bill of Sexual Rights and Responsibilities."[36] We see the Reality Principle at work in *Humanae Vitae* and again in *Persona Humana*, a document of the Sacred Congregation for the Doctrine of the Faith issued about the same time as the American Humanist document.[37]

Simone de Beauvoir and Sex without Consequences

Without boring you with the details, Simone de Beauvoir envisions a world of sex without consequences. In her thought we find procreative sex as the great enemy of women's liberation.[38] She begins her section on motherhood in *The Second Sex* with a discussion of two ways of avoiding it: birth control and abortion.[39] In her thought we

Davanzo, *Un'etica a difesa della vita* (Milano: Editrice Ancora, 1978).

[36] The document appears in *The Humanist* for Jan/Feb 1976. We shall refer to this American Humanist document as NBSRR. Another document that may be fashioned along similar lines is The International Planned Parenthood Federation's *Charter on Sexual and Reproductive Rights*, approved in 1995.

[37] *Persona Humana* was issued on December 29, 1975. Cf. W. B. Skrzydlewski, "Conflict and Schism in Moral Theology and Sexual Ethics," *Homiletic and Pastoral Review* 85 May (1985), pp. 23–32, 48–50.

[38] Here is Beauvoir sounding like Nietzsche: "A woman who expends her energy, who has responsibilities, who knows how harsh is the struggle against the world's opposition, needs – like the male – not only to satisfy her physical desires but also to enjoy the relaxation and diversion provided by agreeable sexual adventures" (*The Second Sex*, p. 646). See my *No Higher Court* for other texts as well.

[39] For more on this, see my "Abortion's Mother: Early Works

find clear evidence of the Pleasure Principle at work: heterosexual, homosexual, and bisexual sexual activity; it makes no difference; it is enough that the urge is there. Such a position is sound bite heaven: "If it feels good, do it!"

The Right to Sexual Expression

One of the clearest expressions of the Pleasure Principle is found in the American Humanist Association's "A New Bill of Sexual Rights and Responsibilities." We read in the introduction to that document:

> "Although we consider marriage, where viable, a cherished human relationship, we believe that other sexual relationships also are significant. In any case, human beings should have the right to express their sexual desires and enter into relationships as they see fit, as long as they do not harm others or interfere with their rights to sexual expression."[40]

And again:

> "We wish to affirm and support the statement of the United Nations World Health Organization on human sexuality: 'Every person has the right to receive sexual information and to consider accepting sexuality for pleasure as well as for procreation'" [section 4].

In a section which treats childhood sexuality, the authors comment:

> "The joy of touching, of giving and receiving affection, and the satisfaction of intimate body responsiveness is the right of everyone throughout life" [section 8].

of Simone de Beauvoir," *Faith and Reason*, 20/4 (1994), pp. 327–46.

[40] Even the authors of NBSRR are reluctant to endorse some forms of sexual expression – sadomasochism, prostitution, and fetishism – though they are quick to add that we should not be all that judgmental.

And in the conclusion to the document we read:

"We human beings are embarking on a wondrous adventure. For the first time we realize that we own our own bodies.[41] Until now our bodies have been in bondage to church or state, which have dictated how we could express our sexuality.[42] We have not been permitted to experience the pleasure and joy of the human body and our sensory nature to their full capacity. [para.] In order to realize our potential for joyful sexual expression, we need to adopt the doctrine that actualizing pleasures are among the highest moral goods – so long as they are experienced with responsibility and mutuality."[43]

The Reality Principle

The constant teaching of the Christian tradition regarding human sexual expression runs counter to the Pleasure Principle.[44] Not that pleasure is not a part of human sexuality, mind you, just that it is meant to be a servant of human beings and not their master.[45]

[41] This is precisely the point warned about in paragraph 17 of *Humane Vitae*.

[42] Perhaps the authors are referring to this passage from scripture: "Your body, you know, is the temple of the Holy Spirit, who is in you since you have received him from God. You are not your own property; you have been bought and paid for. That is why you should use your body for the glory of God" (1 Cor 6:19–20).

[43] There is toward the end of the document a text that should cause us to reflect. Talking of the social meaning of the uninhibited sexual lifestyle urged in the document, the authors claim: "It is quite impossible to have a meaningful, ecstatic sexual and sensual life and to be indifferent to or uncaring about other human beings" [NBSRR, conclusion].

[44] One author who would like to see a reappraisal of the tradition on the point of pleasure is Albert Plé, O.P., *Duty Or Pleasure? A New Appraisal Of Christian Ethics*, trans. M.J. O'Connell (New York: Paragon House Publishers, 1987).

[45] I have always been struck by the passage found in the

In continuing to uphold the link of the unitive and the procreative, in keeping love and life together, the Church tells her sons and daughters, indeed, all of humanity, that there are certain norms in the human sexual arena. Since the possibility of illusion is great in this area, it is most important to be clear that some acts are good or bad of their very nature, and the human person is able to know what these actions are. Fornication, adultery, and contraception are all violations of the prime directive of sexual ethics – keep love and life together – a directive that serves to safeguard the proper roles of the spouses and God in human procreation.

The Church's teaching on human sexuality is one geared to the truth of the human being and the God who creates: the Church's teaching is based on the nature of reality, both human and divine, both objective and subjective. Human sexuality is to be exercised in such a way that it is attuned to the structure of reality; indeed, human sexuality in God's plan must serve as a reliable experience of amative lifegiving – such is truth's yardstick.

Humanae Vitae and the Future: The Church's Role and Responsibility

Thirty years is a long time to reflect upon a document of twenty-five pages.The entire struggle has been fought over the meaning of two words: *love* and *life*.[46] The heart of the

twentieth lecture of Sigmund Freud, *A General Introduction to Psychoanalysis*: "It is a characteristic common to all the perversions that in them reproduction as an aim is put aside. This is actually the criterion by which we judge whether a sexual activity is perverse – if it departs from reproduction in its aims and pursues the attainment of gratification independently."

[46] Pope Paul VI practiced what he preached about *love* and *life* in the writing of *Humanae Vitae* itself. By my rough count, he mentions *love* thirty-eight times and *life* thirty-seven times in the encyclical.

Church's teaching on human sexual expression: Keep love and life together. You cannot do away with one without changing the nature of the other.[47] The love-making without the openness to life is not the total self-giving love should be; the making of life without the making of love is more technological production than truly human procreation.

The debates regarding *Humanae Vitae* have exacted their toll on many who have become embroiled in the oft-times bitter struggle over Pope Paul VI's last encyclical.[48] Many of the faithful have never heard a priest speak about the encyclical and its message from the pulpit; many priests

---

[47] While known by faith from the beginning of Christianity, how to express this anthropological insight in the language of the men and women of each era is a most formidable task, a point noted by Archbishop Chaput in his recent letter to the faithful of his archdiocese on the truth of the encyclical. One attempt to do this philosophically is that of Martin Rhonheimer, "Contraception, Sexual Behavior, and Natural Lawn – Philosophical Foundation of the Norm of *Humanae Vitae*," *The Linacre Quarterly* 56 (1989), pp. 20–57. We note in passing that it is an axiom of ecological thinking that "You can't do one thing only."

[48] See for example G. Egner, *Contraception vs. Tradition: A Catholic Critique* (New York: Herder and Herder, 1967); Ambrogio Valsecchi, *Controversy: The Birth Control Debate 1958–1968*, Introduction by Gregory Baum, O.S.A. (Washington,D.C.: Corpus Books, 1968); Robert Blair Kaiser, *The Politics of Sex And Religion: A Case History In The Development Of Doctrine, 1962–1984* (Kansas City, MO: Leaven Press, 1985); James R. Kelly, "Residual or Prophetic? The Cultural Fate of Roman Catholic Sexual Ethics of Abortion and Contraception," *Social Thought* 12 (1986), pp. 3–18; John Mahoney, S.J., *The Making Of Moral Theology: A Study Of The Roman Catholic Tradition*, The Martin D'Arcy Memorial Lectures 1981–2 (Oxford: Clarendon Press, 1987); Eugene Kennedy, *Tomorrow's Catholics, Yesterday's Church: The Two Cultures Of American Catholicism* (New York: Harper and Row, 1988); and Robert McClory, *Turning Point: The Inside Story of the Papal Birth*

shy away from the task, fearful of alienating the faithful. We do well to remember that we are dealing with two "lost generations."[49]

Regarding the role and responsibility of the Church, paragraph 31 of *Humanae Vitae* sounds the proper note: Men and women of good will, "We now call you to the splendid work of education and growth in love." Education in love, in the true meaning of that oft-misused four letter word, is to bring *reality* into the important area of human sexuality: the Reliable Experience of Amative Lifegiving Is Truth's Yardstick. Human longing will not be satisfied with anything less, indeed, it cannot. Love and life and the law of God inscribed into the nature of the human person are indeed the measure of what it means truthfully to be human:

> "None can achieve true happiness, the happiness that they desire with the strength of their whole soul, unless they observe the laws inscribed on their nature by the Most High God."[50]

The Resources Available
The Church has a valuable resource for facing the next

Control Commission and How 'Humanae Vitae' Changed the Life of Patty Crowley and the Future of the Church (New York: Crossroad, 1995).

[49] This point is made by Archbishop Chaput in his letter on the truth of the encyclical. The lost generations are his own and his teachers.

[50] The text is from paragraph 31 of *Humanae Vitae*. Janet Smith, *Humanae Vitae: A Challenge to Love* (New Hope, KY: New Hope Publications, n.d.), hits the nail right on the head: "if you are not ready for making babies, you are not ready for sexual intercourse." Christopher Derrick has it in a sound bite: "Sex is about babies." See his *Honest Love and Human Life: Is the Pope Right about Contraception?* (New York: Coward-McCann, 1969), and *Sex and Sacredness: a Catholic Homage to Venus* (San Francisco: Ignatius Press, 1982).

century in the writings of John Paul II. Indeed, it is as if his pontificate has been given to the Church to provide her with the tools to teach the truth of *Humanae Vitae* in the next century.[51] It in his writings that we begin to glimpse in earnest the deep anthropological truths embedded in *Humanae Vitae*. Defenders of the Church's teaching on the inseparable connection of love and life have opened fertile new vistas for theological speculation. Foremost is the elaboration of a theology of the body which was the continuing theme of the Wednesday audiences for several years.[52] In addition this pontiff has written much on the dignity and the role of women, both in the Church and in society as a whole.[53] I would regard John Paul II's elucidation of the foundations of Roman Catholic moral theology in *Veritatis*

---

[51] A good place to begin is Karol Wojtyla, *Love and Responsibility*, trans. H.T. Willetts (New York: Farrar, Strauss, and Giroux, 1981; re-issued by Ignatius Press, 1994). Original Polish edition, *Milosc i Odpowiedzialnosc*, 1960.

[52] Pope John Paul II, *The Theology of the Body: Human Life in the Divine Plan* (Boston: Pauline Books and Media, 1997), also available in CD-Rom format. Is it my imagination or has there been a deafening silence on the part of those who deny the truth of *Humanae Vitae* to discuss John Paul II's theology of the body? One author who thinks so is John S. Grabowski, "'Evangelium Vitae' and 'Humanae Vitae': A Tale of Two Encyclicals," *Homiletic and Pastoral Review* 97/2 (November 1996), pp. 7–15. One author who does discuss the theology of the body is Lisa Sowle Cahill, "Catholic Sexual Ethics and the Dignity of the Person: A Double Message," *Theological Studies* 50 (1989), pp. 120–50. While Cahill professes an appreciation for the pope's personalism, she wonders if the theology of the body is able to handle the expanded notion of 'experience' being advanced by homosexuals and feminists who challenge the Church's perennial teaching regarding human sexual expression as a "monogamous, permanent, procreative, and permanent union."

[53] A good place to begin is with his apostolic letter, *Mulieris Dignitatem*, dated August 15, 1988. This thought continues in John Paul II's "Letter to Women," *Origins* 25 9 (1995), pp. 138–45.

Splendor as crowning his attempt to ready the Church for the third millenium of Christianity.[54]

Going hand in hand with the theology of the body are the pontiff's teachings on the importance of the family, an integral feature of the Church's teaching on the proper use of human sexuality. John Paul II's clearest outline of a strategy for the Church of the 21st century to educate in love regarding the truth of *Humanae Vitae* is found in Familiaris Consortio, a veritable blueprint for living *Humanae Vitae* in the next century.[55] *Humanae Vitae* 16 and *Familiaris Consortio* 33 both urge that the teaching of chastity be based upon a method experienced as reliable in its keeping together the love-making and the life-giving meanings embedded in

[54] Not all share my enthusiasm for the encyclical. See for example Joseph Selling and Jan Jans, eds., *The Splendor of Accuracy: An Examination of the Assertions Made by 'Veritatis Splendor'* (Grand Rapids: Eerdmans, 1994); Richard A. McCormick, S.J., "Some Early Reactions to 'Veritatis Splendor,'" *Theological Studies* 55/3 (1994), pp. 481–506; Michael E. Allsopp and John J. O'Keefe, eds., *Veritatis Splendor: American Responses* (Kansas City, MO: Sheed and Ward, 1995). Cf. James F. Keenan, S.J. and Thomas R. Kopfensteiner, "Moral Theology Out of Western Europe," *Theological Studies* 59/1 (1998), pp. 107–35.

[55] *Familiaris Consortio* was issued on November 22, 1981. See also John Paul II's "Letter to Families" dated February 2, 1994. The emphasis placed on the importance of the family can serve the Church well in the area of ecumenism. Be it the Jewish or Islamic traditions in the West or the religious traditions of the East, the importance of the family for the great monotheistic religions is a sine qua non for an appreciation and an understanding of these faiths. A recent promising initiative of some Protestant churches begun in the American South, "True Love Waits," situates human sexual expression where it should be located: in the heart of the human family. On this point, Christians can agree not only among themselves but with adherents of other faiths as well. While it is true that most of contemporary feminism, once again following the lead of Simone de Beauvoir, is hostile to the family, seeing it as the oppressor of women, we do find among some feminists an appreciation for the communal aspects of reality. While

authentic human sexual expression. Natural Family Planning fills the bill.[56]

On a practical level, may I recommend that one excellent way for the Christian family to be strengthened is for the teaching of Natural Family Planning to be established as a Church-wide policy for all couples as part of their marriage preparations. This teaching of Natural Family Planning must include both its moral theory as well its technical aspects. Because of its dual component, the need for cooperation by the priests and the laity is readily apparent. The appreciation of both for the work of the other may well grow as a result of this collaboration.

NFP and CCL: Reworking Two Acronyms

Time was, Natural Family Planning in the eyes of some

we may not agree with everything that thinkers such as Elizabeth Fox-Genovese and Sara Ruddick and Carol Gilligan have to say about the importance of the family, the interdependence fostered by a recognition of how we are related to each other by relational ties, family ties, if you will, does leave the door open for dialogue on this score as well.

[56] In addition to the work of the Pope Paul VI Institute in Omaha, Nebraska, many of the publications of The Pope John Center, now The National Catholic Bioethics Center, feature articles on Natural Family Planning. Several of these are listed below, along with additional entries: William A. Uricchio and Mary Kay Williams, eds., *Proceedings of a Research Conference on Natural Family Planning* (Washington, DC: The Human Life Foundation, 1973); John and Sheila Kippley, *The Art of Natural Family Planning*, Foreword by Ronald A. Prem, M.D. (Cincinnati: Couple to Couple League International, 1979); Rev. Msgr. James McHugh, S.T.D. and Gerard Brunelle, "The Bishops and Natural Family Planning: Theological and Pastoral Implications," Moral Theology Today (1984), pp. 287–312; Konald A. Prem, M.D., "Family Planning Today: Contraceptive and NFP," in *Reproductive Technologies, Marriage and the Church* (1988), pp. 210–225; R.E.J. Ryder, "Natural Family Planning: Effective Birth Control Supported by the Catholic Church," *British Medical Journal*, September 19 (1993), pp. 723–726; World Health Organization,

meant *Not For Progressives*. Thanks to the labors of the Billings and the Hilgers as well as the many others devoted to this work, we have grown beyond such a narrow view. Natural Family Planning is better understood to suggest *Now and For Posterity*.

The acronym CCL stands for the Couple-to-Couple League. May I commandeer the acronym so that it can also stand for the *Couples to Clergy League* as well? Any meaningful initiative on the values of Natural Family Planning will probably come from the laity to the clergy rather than the other way around. The Second Vatican Council urged the laity to take their rightful place in the Church; *Humanae Vitae*, especially in its regard for the dignity of Christian spouses, helps show the way.[57]

Married couples will have two tasks: 1) They will need enough faith in the science behind Natural Family Planning to show in their lives that it works; and 2) they will have to tell their priests and bishops that contraception is a dead-end.[58] The Church has known this in theory all along. But a

---

Division of Family Health, *Natural Family Planning: What Health Workers Need to Know* (Geneva: World Health Organization, 1995); John H. Geerling, "Natural Family Planning," *American Family Physician* 52/6 (1995), pp. 174–79; and Bob Ryder and Hubert Campbell, "Natural Family Planning in the 1990s," orig. in *The Lancet* (July 22, 1995) reprinted in *Child and Family*, 21/4 (1998), pp. 320–26.

[57] Pope Paul VI says as much in paragraph 26 of Humanae Vitae: "Among the fruits that result from a generous effort of fidelity to the divine law, one of the most precious is that married couples themselves not infrequently feel the desire to communicate their experience to others. Thus a new and most noteworthy form of apostolate of like towards like comes to be included in the vast field of the vocation of the laity: it is married couples themselves who become apostles and guides to other married couples. Among so many forms of apostolate, this is assuredly one of those that seem most opportune today."

[58] The link between the birth control pill and its ability to cause early abortions is one way in which the contraceptive men-

generation of priests has had it drummed into them that Natural Family Planning is nothing else but a new name for "rhythm" and that it does not work effectively.[59] These priests have read in the dissenting theologians and their daily newspapers and heard on the TV newscasts and talk shows that only the Pill and the condom and the IUD and the diaphragm and the tubal ligations and the vasectomies and the abortions are what "the people in the pews" are living.[60] If Catholics want to hear sermons from the pulpit

tality is truly a dead-end. For more see Joseph W. Goldzieher, M.D., *Hormonal Contraception: Pills, Injections, and Implants* (Dallas: Essential Medical Information Systems, 1989); Nicholas Tonti-Filippini, "The Pill: Abortifacient or Contraceptive? A Literature Review," *The Linacre Quarterly* 62/1 (February 1995), pp. 4–28; Lawrence F. Roberge, M.S., "Abortifacient Vaccines: Technological Update and Christian Appraisal," in John N. Kilner, M. de S. Cameron and D. Schiedermayer, eds., *Bioethics and the Future of Medicine: A Christian Appraisal*, A Horizons in Bioethics Book (Grand Rapids: Eerdmans, n.d.), pp. 178–186; and Thomas J. O'Donnell, S.J., *Medicine and Christian Morality*, 3rd revised and updated edition (Staten Island: Alba House, 1996), p. 44.

[59] According to Richard A. McCormick, Richard, S.J., *The Critical Calling: Reflections on Moral Dilemmas Since Vatican II* (Washington, DC: Georgetown University Press, 1989), p. 280: "Discovering whether natural family planning 'works' means running an irresponsible risk."

[60] The recent FDA approval (September 2, 1998) of the "Emergency Contraception Kit" is the latest attempt to sell early abortion under the flag of contraception. This feat of semantic gymnastics has been accomplished by redefining "pregnancy" from conception until implantation. In the 4th edition (1994) of *Mosby's Medical Dictionary*, p. 1263, "pregnancy" is defined as "the gestational process, comprising the growth and development within a woman of a new individual from conception through the embryonic and fetal periods to birth." In the 20th edition of *Williams Obstetrics* (1997), p. 19, we read: "Fertilization of the human ovum by a spermatozoan [sic] occurs in the fallopian tube within a short time (minutes to at most a few hours after

once again on moral subjects that matter to couples who want to live their faith, it is up to the couples to tell the priests that Natural Family Planning works and that the devices of the sexual revolution are all dead-ends.[61]

Most priests I know are extremely conscientious and have great love for the people entrusted to their care. Even when convinced of the truth of natural family planning, many priests will consider themselves ill-prepared to for the details of the method. This too will be the work of Christian married couples. When the abstinence that is an

---

ovulation) and 6 days after fertilization, the blastocyst begins to implant in the endometrium, and pregnancy has begun." Linguistic legerdemain notwithstanding, the Catholic defense of human life begins at the moment of conception, a point stated in paragraph 51 of *Gaudium et Spes*: "God, the Lord of life, has entrusted to humanity the noble mission of safeguarding life, and men and women must carry it out in a manner worthy of themselves. Life must be protected with the utmost care from the moment of conception: abortion and infanticide are abominable crimes." The text is referred to in Humanae Vitae 14 and reappears in the *Declaration on Procured Abortion, Donum Vitae*, and *The Gospel of Life*.

[61] In addition to the scholarly treatments upholding the truth of the Church's teaching on human sexual expression, several popular titles should be mentioned as well: Rev. H. Vernon Sattler, C.Ss.R., Sex Education in the Catholic Family, Common Faith Tract no. 8 (Front Royal, VA: Christendom Publications, 1984); Richard M. Hogan, The Wonder of Human Sexuality (St. Paul, MN: The Leaflet Missal Company, 1985); Paul M. Quay, S.J., PhD, The Christian Meaning of Human Sexuality (San Francisco: Ignatius Press, 1985); Rev. Richard J. Rego, The True Meaning of Love: The Beauty and Wisdom of Church Teaching (St. Paul, MN: The Leaflet Missal Company, 1990); Ruth S. Taylor, MD, Ann Nerbun, MSN, and Rev. R. Hogan, Our Power to Love: God's Gift of Our Sexuality (San Francisco: Ignatius Press, 1991); Thomas and Donna Finn, Intimate Bedfellows: Love, Sex, and the Catholic Church (Boston: St. Paul Books and Media, 1993); and George Sim Johnston, "The Intelligent Engaged Couple's Guide to Sex and Family Planning," Child and Family 21/4 (1998), pp. 313–19.

integral part of Natural Family Planning becomes difficult, perhaps here is where the spouses can look to their priests for aid and comfort. In this regard, the CCL will function as a *Clergy to Couple League*. The need for a Christian community of faith to face these issues together is also an instance of building up the family of faith.

Several years ago I took a course in Natural Family Planning, unaccompanied save for my good intentions. I attended along with approximately fifteen couples, affectionately dubbed the "granola crowd." Such efforts in dioceses around the country must continue, to be sure, but the ability to add to the Natural Family Planning lectures the theological roots of *Humanae Vitae* 16 and *Familiaris Consortio* 33 must be stressed. Without this theological component, Natural Family Planning can come across as part of the contraceptive mentality rather than as a way in which spouses can honor God with their bodies as they "fight for the work of God."

Conclusion

Which will it be: will we sit with the young ladies from Smith College chanting "Our bodies, our lives, our right to decide" as the priests enter the hall? Will ours be the thought of the character in Edna O'Brien's novel as we live in our lives the thought she expressed: "Oh God, who does not exist, you hate women, otherwise you'd have made them different." Or rather will our attitude be that of a different prayer: "Oh God who does exist, you love men and women and that's why you made us the way we are." Let the dissenters continue to think that *Humanae Vitae* is the birth control encyclical. We know it is much more: *Humanae Vitae* is a fight for the work of God. My brothers and sisters, We are that work; my brothers and sisters, that fight is ours. "God is Lord of life and death, we the in-between."

FAITH AND THE
THERAPEUTIC CULTURE

William Kilpatrick

Seventeen years ago I wrote a book about the dangers of mixing psychology with religious faith.[1] Such a mixing, I cautioned, would result in a dilution of faith. Six years before that, Paul Vitz had made a similar point: psychology, he wrote, had become a substitute religion – a religion that encouraged a cult of self-worship.[2] We both emphasized that this psychological faith, although it bore a surface resemblance to Christianity, was incompatible with Christian faith, indeed, deeply hostile to it.

The psychological faith has proven to be a sturdy creed. Almost all of the criticisms we made then could be made today. The concepts of popular psychology are still being blended with Christian faith, and confusion still abounds. The psychological attraction is not, of course, confined to the area of religion. Psychology has had a profound influence on the rest of society, as well. The assumptions and techniques of psychology and therapy have found their way into business, into schools, into families, into popular entertainment, and even into the courts – so much so, that it has become common to speak of our society as a therapeutic culture. As long ago as 1966 Philip Rieff predicted that this therapeutic mode of organizing society and identities would triumph over all other modes. It would

[1] William K. Kilpatrick, *Psychological Seduction* (Nashville: Thomas Nelson, 1983).

[2] Paul C. Vitz, *Psychology as Religion* (Grand Rapids: Wm. B. Eerdmans, 1997).

become the frame of reference by which all other beliefs and commitments would be judged.[3]

It stands to reason that Christian churches ought to resist this rival faith. Instead, they have in differing degrees been seduced by it, unable in many cases to say where the psychological faith ends and the Christian faith begins. I thought this blending of psychology and faith was a dangerous thing when I first addressed the issue, and I think it's a danger now. So I'd like to offer some of the arguments for avoiding this ill-advised ecumenism. The arguments fall roughly into two categories: arguments of the don't-embarrass-yourself variety, and the more serious arguments of the don't-cut-your-own-throat variety.

The first line of criticism was suggested to me by a recent article by Paul Vitz titled "Support from psychology for the fatherhood of God."[4] He first notes that the Christian concept of God as Father has been under attack – much of the attack coming from Catholics influenced by feminist psychology. But, says Vitz, much of this psychology, based as it is on an androgynous view of the person, is passé. All the latest research, he continues, shows how very different the sexes are, and how fathers and mothers play distinct roles which are not interchangeable. All the statistics, moreover, clearly demonstrate what happens when fathers cease playing their role in family and society. Indeed, fatherlessness correlates with crime, drug addiction, school dropout rates and out-of-wedlock pregnancies better than any other factor. Moreover, it turns out that boys are much more fragile than girls and suffer much more acutely from the absence of fathers.[5] Vitz observes:

It seems to me bizarre to the point of pathology at this

[3] Philip Rieff, *The Triumph of the Therapeutic* (Harmondsworth: Penguin Books, 1966).

[4] Paul C. Vitz, "Support from Psychology for the Fatherhood of God," *Homiletic and Pastoral Review* 97/5 (Feb. 1997).

[5] See, for example, psychologist Michael Gurian's two books on the subject, *The Wonder of Boys* and *A Fine Young Man*.

time in our culture to be trying to remove God the Father from our theology. We are just now aware of the widespread social pathology, especially the increase in violence, resulting from fatherlessness in families – and the data are staggering![6] What worse moment could there be to diminish fatherhood in our theology? We have enough absent fathers without trying to send God the Father away too! To remove God the Father is to remove a major support for positive male identity. In a church that is already far more popular with women than with men, this means the removal of one of the few remaining supports for men.[7]

Meanwhile, says Vitz, the religion of Islam, which does acknowledge the importance of fathers, is probably the most rapidly growing of the world's religions. "Recently," writes Vitz, "I heard a report that black Baptist women were urging their husbands to become Muslims because they thought their men should have a religion and thought Christianity to be inadequate for men."[8]

The point, of course, is that when Christians embrace psychological fads they often end up behind the curve when newer and better research come to the fore. Just how far behind the curve is suggested by a Christian youth curriculum which includes a cross dressing activity called the "Suitcase Relay." It works like this: "On the word GO, a first couple (boy and girl) from each team must run with their suitcase to the opposite end of the room, open the suitcase, and put on everything in the suitcase. . . . The boy putting on the ladies dress and the girl putting on the man's suit."[9]

[6] See Blankenhorn, *Fatherless America*: Confronting our Most Urgent Social Problem, 1995.

[7] *Ibid.*, p. 13.

[8] *Ibid.*, p. 14.

[9] Lyman Coleman, *Hassles* (Littleton, Colorado: Serendipity House, 1994), p. 4.

To the creators of such curriculums there is only one thing to say that might be effective: "Stop! Don't embarrass yourself! Psychologists no longer counsel gender confusion. Sex roles, they have found, are not to be carelessly tampered with."

One can point to a number of other therapeutic concepts which are now either in disgrace or in dispute with professionals but are nevertheless still tremendously popular with religious educators, parishes, priests and bishops. Take the concept of self-esteem. It's a central element in curricula for Catholic and other Christian youth. Yet in psychological circles serious questions are being raised about the efficacy of high self-esteem, and about whether the trait can even be measured. For example, the measure of self-esteem used in the well-known AAUW study seems highly dubious. According to that study girls suffer a sharp drop in self-esteem when they enter high schools. But look at the items employed on the self-esteem questionnaire: questions such as "I'm happy the way I am," "I like most things about myself" and "I'm an important person." To these questions children can choose one of five responses "always true," "sort of true," "sometimes true/sometimes false," "sort of false" or "always false."[10] But what sort of person would answer "always true" to "I'm happy the way I am" or "I'm an important person?" Someone with good self-insight or someone who feels a need to be defensive or boastful? It's not surprising that boys, who are less self-reflective than girls of the same age, would score higher on this test. Moreover, as Christina Hoff Sommers has pointed out there seems to be no connection between high self-esteem scores and academic success. A little reported outcome of the AAUW study is that, although boys tested higher than girls on self-esteem, the very highest average scores were

[10] *Expectations and Aspirations: Gender Roles and Self-Esteem* (Washington, D.C.: American Association of University Women, 1990). Cited in Christina Hoff Sommers, *Who Stole Feminism* (New York: Simon & Schuster, 1994) pp. 145–46.

obtained by black girls and black boys. When the results were broken down by race, black boys showed the highest level of self-esteem. Yet, as is well-known, black boys do not, on the average, do well in school, and they do not go on in very large numbers to college. On the other hand, white girls – the group that scores lowest on self-esteem – is the group that displays the greatest academic success.[11]

These findings should at least raise doubts about the importance of self-esteem, but there's more. Recent studies by Roy Baumeister of Case Western Reserve University suggest that high self-esteem may be related to anti-social behavior. In fact, the most dangerous youth seem to have highly inflated opinions of themselves. Efforts to raise self-esteem, suggests Baumeister, may actually increase violent behavior.

Once again, Christian educators seem to be off on the wrong track. At just the moment in our history when youth violence and drug use is at an all time high, at just the moment when adults ought to be talking to youngsters about self-control and self restraint, their energies are focused instead on teaching children to applaud themselves. We seem bent on giving our children the opposite of what they need.

It's the same with the popular concept of non-judgmentalism. If there was ever a time in which it was important for youngsters to exercise good judgment this is it. As psychologist William Coulson has pointed out, "It's precisely the necessity of judgment, not its absence, that must be promoted with the young today, given the magnitude of the drug problem."[12] Yet, in Christian education the emphasis is still very often on acceptance, trust and the absence of judgment. A good example is provided in a curriculum lesson for evangelical children. The lesson presents two children, Amanda, who is fat and unattractive, and Jason, who

[11] Sommers, *Ibid.*, p. 149.

[12] W.R. Coulson, Memorandum to the Federal Drug Education Curricula Panel, April 23, 1988, p. 1.

shows a marijuana joint around school to impress the other boys. The lesson is that students are not to judge either Amanda or Jason, but rather "to accept them as they are."[13] Cathy Mickels and Audrey McKeever, authors of a book on psychologized Christian education, pinpoint the problem. They write, "To equate a girl who is quiet and unattractive with a boy showing an illegal drug around is not only confusing, but is an example of distorted and twisted reasoning."[14] As the authors point out, Jason is probably not the kind of boy you would want your child to associate with, yet there is nothing in the curriculum to indicate that he ought to be avoided or corrected. In 1 Corinthians 15: 33 we are told, "Do not be deceived: bad company corrupts good morals," but the world of Christian textbooks does not usually encourage this sort of judgment. Rather, it is a world inhabited by basically good and well-intentioned people who seem to have been barely touched by the effects of Original Sin.

Examples of this sort can be multiplied. Charles Sykes, in his book, A Nation of Victims, describes a Colorado church which offers thirteen different weekly support groups ranging from "Debtors Anonymous" through "Sex and Love Addicts Anonymous" to "Codependents of Sex Addicts Anonymous."[15] Evidently this parish subscribes to the medical model of human behavior. Meanwhile, other churches have bought into the notion that homosexuality is biologically driven and is therefore not a choice. Yet these

[13] *The Gospel According to St. Bernard,* compiled and edited by the Zig Ziglar Corporation, produced and distributed by Christian Video Enterprises (Plantation, Florida: Christian Video Enterprises, Inc., 1992) Lesson Number Two.

[14] Cathy Mickels and Audrey McKeever, "Spiritual Junk Food: The Dumbing Down of Christian Youth" (unpublished manuscript available through Eagle Forum of Washington, 413 B 19th St., Suite 129, Lynden, Washington 98264, Tel. (360) 354–6035) p. 263.

[15] Charles J. Sykes, *A Nation of Victims* (New York: St. Martins Press, 1992), pp. 135–36.

are issues which are hotly contested by professional psychologists. For example, the evidence that homosexuality is biologically driven is quite skimpy and far from convincing. In any event it seems quite ill-advised for Christians to join the chorus of theories that suggest that we can't help ourselves, that we're not really responsible for our behavior.

Another episode which should be embarrassing to Christians is the informal alliance formed between evangelical Christians and clinical psychologists during the day care witch hunts of the 1980s. The psychologists had come up with a number of interesting concepts which soon gained the force of law. One ironclad law asserted that children never lie about sex; another claimed that repressed memories could be reliably recovered. More ominously, the psychologists had discovered a new syndrome called "Ritual Satanic Child Abuse." The symptoms of this disease were legion and included forced sex, occult rituals and animal sacrifice. Unfortunately, many evangelicals in the affected localities were all too ready to believe that Satan was alive and active in the local day care centers. In many instances they joined forces with the psychologists and law enforcers, and even provided incriminating evidence against the defendants. Dozens of individuals ended up in prison as a result of the day care scares of the Eighties, careers and reputations were ruined. We know now that it really was a witch hunt. The FBI reports that there is no evidence of a single case of ritual Satanic child abuse in the United States. We know now that the child witnesses had been subjected to leading questions, threats and bribes. We know now that most of the testimony was bizarre and fantastic. We know now that, in addition to recovered memories, there are also suggested memories – memories of events that never happened. Thankfully, most of the convictions in these cases have now been overturned, but many individuals still linger in prison. The day care cases show that child experts can sometimes be extremely naïve, and that Christians can sometimes be remarkably gullible. None of this should surprise us, nor should it be surprising that when the two join forces the result may simply be credulity compounded.

It's embarrassing to be behind the times, and even more embarrassing to be caught up in psychological delusions and hysterias, but embarrassment ought not be the only reason for avoiding ill-considered alliances with the world of psychology. There are reasons of survival, too – reasons of the don't-cut-your-own-throat variety. The mixing of psychology with faith sometimes resembles suicidal behavior, and this is especially true when questions of doctrine are involved. Indeed, as should be apparent by now the distinction between what is merely embarrassing, and what is suicidal is hard to maintain. For example, dabbling with the idea of God the Mother while young men all over the world are flocking to the religion of Islam is a gravely serious matter. The feminization of Christian churches is not just an embarrassment it's a dangerous experiment.

One of the most dangerous consequences of carelessly mixing therapy with faith is a diminished sense of sin. The best evidence that this has already happened in the Catholic Church is the tremendous drop-off in the practice of confession over the last thirty years. When we couple this with the nearly hundred percent communion turnout in most parishes, we have to conclude that most parishioners don't have a strong consciousness of sin. They seem to have been so schooled in the gospel of self-acceptance that they can't think of any sins to confess.

A colleague at Boston College told me a story which reinforces the point. He once asked his philosophy class to write an anonymous essay about a personal struggle over right and wrong, good and evil. Most of the students however, were unable to complete the assignment. "Why," he asked. "Well," they said – and apparently this was said without irony – " We haven't done anything wrong." We can see a lot of self-esteem here, but perhaps, not too much self-awareness, certainly very little awareness of sin – a strange absence when one considers that most of these students have had years of Catholic schooling.

Where do such attitudes come from? The conditioning begins at an early age. My five- year old grandson came home from Sunday school one day wearing a badge on which was printed the words "St. Christopher." His teacher had told him he was a saint. So were the other boys and girls in his class. Well, to paraphrase the words of a well-known politician, "I know Christopher, and he's no saint." I suppose this premature canonization is designed to make Christopher and his classmates feel good about themselves, but the effect is to shortcut the whole process of Christian struggle and transformation. It's like drawing a "get out of jail free" card in Monopoly. Or, more accurately, "bank error in your favor, collect $200."

The trouble, once again, is that this inability to talk about sin, along with the inability to talk about Satan and the existence of evil, comes at a time when the imagination of young people is captivated by bands such as KISS (Knights In Satan's Service) and by performers such as Marilyn Manson (who also considers himself a knight in Satan's service). If Christian youth are to struggle against the temptation to evil in this world, they at least ought to be forewarned that evil exists. They ought to know also, that Satan is more than just a name dreamed up by a rock band.

A diminished sense of sin is one problem that results from freely mixing faith with psychology. Another is a diminished sense of the sacred. When I first addressed the issue of psychologized texts for Catholic students I made the following observation: "The constant references to "communications breakdowns," "risk-taking," "involvement," "decision-making," "personhood," "I-you relationships," "getting in touch," "self-disclosure," "awareness," and "assertiveness" carries the implication that all the deep mysteries of faith can be encompassed in secular/psychological categories. In fact, there is very little sense that there are any deep mysteries – that there might be elements of the faith so awesome and unfathomable that they exist far beyond the reach of the social sciences."[16]

One of the deep mysteries that has suffered is the mystery of Christ's presence in the Eucharist. Earlier I suggested that a diminished sense of sin among Catholics may help to explain why so many seem so comfortable about receiving communion without any prior confession. Another explanation is that the sense of awe or reverence over receiving the Body and Blood of Christ has slackened. A poll of Catholics conducted a few years ago revealed that sixty-five percent do not, in fact, believe in the Real Presence. It's an astonishing statistic. And it certainly helps to explain why Catholics have become more casual about communion.

Philip Rieff has written that a therapeutic society is by its very nature a negation of the sacred order. It has no room for the concept of transcendence. Obsessed with self-fulfillment and self-realization, it is uncomfortable with higher claims on our attention. "Religious man was born to be saved, "writes Rieff, "psychological man is born to be pleased."[17] One way of pleasing him is to reduce everything to his size. Religious educators have become rather good at this. In religious studies curricula, both Catholic and evangelical, a great deal of energy goes into entertaining the student with games, puzzles, fun activities and the like. The texts contain happy faces and sad faces, connect-the- dot games, teddy bears, pictures to color, and stickers to paste. One curriculum for evangelical children is entitled "The Gospel According to St. Bernard." It features, as you might guess, a cuddly St. Bernard dog. Here is Berny's Theme Song which introduces each video:

The questions of life are tough to figure
But we found a friend, like us, but bigger

---

[16] Kilpatrick, *Psychological Seduction*, p. 179.
[17] Rieff, *The Triumph*, p. 22.

He helps when we're caught off guard
Here comes the Gospel According to Saint Bernard.
Bernie loves kids like you and me
His doghouse is Florida by the sea
He helps us follow God's plan
When we listen to Bernie
It's never very hard
To love him, he's Bernie
The Saint Bernard.[18]

Just to show how user friendly Bernie is, the authors of the curriculum preface the series with the following admonition: "You will find that children view the series differently than adults. As an example, adults expect the voice of Bernie to be deep and resonate, but children want to hear a friendly voice that speaks to them on their own level, not a voice of authority."[19]

The quest for relevance does not abate as students grow older. For high school and junior high students there are blind walks, trust falls, tree hugging exercises, role playing, self-esteem relays, and various touching activities such as the "blush" game and the "lap-sit" game.[20] Besides taking away valuable time that might be spent learning Christian doctrine, the use of such games carries the implication that the Christian faith by itself is insufficient. Students may be forgiven if they gain the impression that the faith lacks power to stand by itself; that it must be reinforced by secular concepts and activities; that it must be made attractive by blending it with secular forms of entertainment.

More insidiously, such presentations subtly erode the sense of awe and reverence with which God ought to be approached. In their quest for what is relevant and recog-

[18] The Gospel According to St. Bernard, Theme Song, vv. 1 and 4.

[19] Christian Video Enterprises, Inc., Promotional materials for *The Gospel According to St. Bernard* 2/11 (1997).

[20] Mickels and McKeever, "Spiritual Junk Food," pp. 66, 111.

nizable, religious educators often reduce God to a comfortable size. He becomes a chummy friend who we can approach with an easy and casual familiarity. Thus, even for those Catholics who still believe in the real presence of Christ in the Eucharist, receiving communion need not be an occasion of soul searching or prior purification.

This desacralization process can happen even when materials are free of doctrinal error, and even when sound concepts and accurate Bible narratives are present. A lot depends on the presentation. For example, compare the *Faith and Life* series published by Ignatius Press with the Sadlier Series.[21] Book One of Sadlier covers approximately the same content as Book One of *Faith and Life*. The Creation is there, and so is the Fall, the birth of Christ, the Last Supper, Pentecost, the Mass, the Sacrament of Baptism, the Our Father and the Hail Mary. But it's revealing to see what else is in Sadlier. In addition to Jesus, Mary and Joseph and the apostles there is a poem about a fish named Sharkey and a crab named Charlie, a picture of a T-Shirt to be colored in with the signs of Easter joy, a poem about Shelly Turtle and her friends, Gator and Froggie, a connect-the-dots game, a "celebration circles" game, a puzzle to be cut out and glued together, instructions for making a moon and stars mobile, two pages of stickers and a paste-your-picture in a sunflower activity.

The average child of course, is familiar with all this. He has encountered similar activities and games in countless other places. And there's the rub. The continual juxtaposition of the sacred and the secular conveys the, hopefully unintended, message that the two are on the same level. The authors seem afraid to suggest that there is anything outside or beyond the child's experience. Over and over, the events depicted in the Bible are related to everyday and often trivial activities. The illustrations convey the same

---

[21] *Our Heavenly Father*, Faith and Life Series: Book One (San Francisco: Ignatius Press, 1987); Coming to God, Coming to Faith Program: Book One (New York: William H. Sadlier, Inc., 1995).

message. Most of them depict boys and girls engaged in everyday activities: drinking milk, feeding a cat, shaking hands, playing ball, playing at the seashore, blowing pinwheels, flying kites, and so forth – exactly the same sort of illustrations that children would find in a public school text.

By contrast the cover of Book One of the *Faith and Life* Series is graced by Raphael's "Creation of the Animals." In this painting God the Creator has a kindly countenance but at the same time He appears immensely powerful, and He dwarfs the lion standing beside Him. The painting evokes a response of awe and humility.

The rest of the text is illustrated with more Raphael's, as well as paintings by Fra Angelico, Barocci, Titian, Velasquez and Veronese. The sections on the Mass and the sacrament of Baptism are accompanied by photos of a priest reverently saying Mass and administering the sacrament. There are no distracting pictures of boys and girls flying kites, no teddy bears, no fun activities, no stickers to paste. The chapters are short, readable, and present in an understandable sequence the story of Creation, Fall, preparation for the Savior, and the birth, death and resurrection of Christ – in short, that powerful and eternally relevant story which changed the world, and which has never needed a supporting cast of stuffed animals and cartoon characters.

The text, though simplified, does not pander to the child's immaturity, nor does it convey the notion that the mysteries of faith are comprehensible from within the child's own experience. On the contrary, the refusal to compromise with fads and gimmicks and self-esteem activities, allows the drama of redemption to shine through as the unique and central event that it is.

It would be a mistake, however, to focus too narrowly on catechisms and their influence. It is not only the catechisms that have become psychologized, it is our whole culture. In 1966 Philip Rieff predicted the triumph of the therapeutic in our society.

A therapeutic culture, he observed, is one which is focused primarily on the self and the needs, both material and psychological, of the self. A therapeutic society is not simply one in which many people go to therapists, but rather one in which the therapeutic mode of analysis becomes the preferred way of explaining what life is all about, and the therapeutic technique is extended to all areas of life. The most obvious examples of this therapeutic expansion are the television talk shows which serve as mass therapies of confession, and which attract a huge viewing audience. Such entertainments should not distract us, however, from noticing that the therapeutic is essentially a religion, a religion in which faith in God is replaced by faith in the self and its possibilities. The therapeutic can tolerate other religions as long as they conform to its own image and likeness, but it is implacably hostile to religions which make a transcendent or supernatural claim. The message of the therapeutic faith is nearly the reverse of John the Baptist's message, "He must increase and I must decrease." It's central creed is nicely captured in the words of the first Humanist Manifesto issued in 1933 by the American Humanist Association: "Religious humanism considers the complete realization of human personality to be the end of man's life and seeks its development and fulfillment in the here and now."[22] This, as the advertisers might say, is not your father's religion. "The modern individual," writes Rieff, "can only use the community as the necessary stage for his effort to enhance himself."[23] In a similar way many individuals now look upon religion as simply a useful servant of the self. In commenting on the theology of Harvey Cox, James Hitchcock writes:

> The religious man of the late twentieth century is someone 'open' to practically every religious practice

[22] *Humanist Manifestoes I and II* (Buffalo, N.Y.: Prometheus Books, 1973), pp. 7–11.

[23] Rieff, *The Triumph*, p. 45.

or discipline, but only to the degree that they seem to enhance his subjective sense of well-being. Whereas practically all the religions of the worlds have demanded that the individual submit himself to something greater than himself, [Harvey] Cox reverses the process. The individual becomes the final test of everything, and all religion is subordinated to the authority of the self seeking infinite gratification.[24]

A few lines later Hitchcock makes the point more succinctly:

The older secularism was hostile to religion and sought to destroy it. The newer secularism often now destroys the soul of religion while keeping its body.[25]

The co-opting of religion by the therapeutic begins simply enough. In curricula for Christian youth it begins with the incessant repetition of the word "you." "How do you feel...? "What do you think . . .?" "Do you like to . . .? "Tell something you will do . . ."

The co-opting culminates in spectacles like the one which surrounded the death of Princess Diana. Faced with the stark contrast between the lives of Mother Theresa and Princess Di, the masses concluded that both were saints. Mother Theresa's project in life was to do God's work, Diana's project was mainly herself. For years we were treated to open displays of her affairs, her emotions, her sufferings, her illnesses, her charities, her wardrobe, and her confessions. In an earlier age such a life might have elicited responses of pity or contempt, but in a therapeutic culture these are exactly the traits that merit sainthood.

Of course, the best example of the therapeutic co-opting religion is provided for us by Bill Clinton. It is a marvel to see how easily and smoothly he mixes the therapeutic mode with the religious mode, and how effortlessly and

[24] James Hitchcock, *What is Secular Humanism?* (Ann Arbor: Servant Books, 1982), pp. 77–78.

[25] *Ibid.*, p. 79.

shamelessly he bends the vocabulary of faith to serve his own designs. He has "sinned," he seeks "forgiveness," he has a "broken spirit." Peggy Noonan reports that after losing his re-election race for governor in 1980, Clinton changed his strategy: "Knowing the people of Arkansas had come to see him as different, as too liberal and too Yale, he immediately went out and joined the only local church choir that sang on TV every Sunday morning. People liked it. He manipulated them for gain, to win. And in 1982 he won."[26] In a recent issue of the *Wall Street Journal*, Dick Morris, Clinton's former advisor, is quoted as saying, "The people who are going to help [Mr. Clinton] out of this scandal are ministers, clergymen, psychiatrists and experts on addiction."[27] Shortly afterwards *Newsweek* reported that President Clinton had asked a trio of ministers to be his personal "accountability group."[28] One of them is the Rev. J. Philip Wogaman who thinks the President should not resign or be impeached. According to *Newsweek*, Wogaman believes that such demands would be judgmental because all men are sinners. The article is immediately followed by a related boxed article reflecting the opinion of therapists. They endorse the ministerial "accountability group" but say Clinton also needs therapy for his "sex addiction." As one of the therapists puts it, "If he can admit his problem and share it with people, he can leave a very powerful legacy of healing."[29] It is very strange, this spectacle of ministers and therapists joining forces to heal the President. It is difficult to say what will come of it, but I suspect that it is the forces of religion that have the most to lose from the alliance.

[26] Peggy Noonan, "American Caligula," *Wall Street Journal* (Sept. 14, 1998).

[27] Sally Satel, "Is Clinton Out of Control?" *Wall Street Journal* (Sept. 20, 1998).

[28] Kenneth Woodward, "The Road to Repentance," *Newsweek* (Sept. 28, 1998), pp. 44–6.

[29] Lynette Clementson and Pat Wingert, "Clinton on the Couch," *Newsweek* (Sept. 28, 1998), p. 46.

Some forty years ago, C.S. Lewis wrote, "If Christianity is untrue, no honest man will want to believe it, however helpful it might be; if it is true, every honest man will want to believe it, even if it gives him no help at all."[30] In a psychological society, however, the question of the truth of religion is beside the point. The main question, the only question, really, is the question of whether or not religion furthers the cause of the self.

It's important for people of faith to keep this in mind, because it means that there can be no real compromise between Christianity and the psychological society. Philip Rieff is quite adamant about this. In a 1991 essay he claims that the therapeutic culture (which he now calls the "Third world culture") is at war with traditional culture, and aims to destroy it.[31] This seems overblown at first. If the therapeutic culture is our enemy it appears to be a rather tame enemy. After all it speaks the language of compassion, sensitivity and tolerance. But any culture which has no use for truth is ultimately a dangerous culture. If there is no meaning outside the self, there is no meaning. And if there is no meaning there is no morality. The most profound statement on the subject comes from Dostoevsky who warned us, "If there is no God everything is permissible." To put the matter flatly, the therapeutic culture has no God. It is well on the way to dismantling the moral structure of society through touting concepts such as addiction and biological determinism, and by semi-sincere appeals to tolerance, compassion and diversity. And there is no reason to think it will put limits on what is morally permissible. In the end, there is not a dimes worth of difference between the nihilism of the therapeutic culture and the nihilism of a

[30] C.S. Lewis, "Man or Rabbit?" in *God in the Dock* (Grand Rapids: Eerdmans, 1970), pp. 108–9.

[31] Philip Rieff, "The Newer Noises of War in the Second Culture Camp," *Yale Journal of Law and the Humanities* 3 (1991), pp. 315–88.

Nietzsche – except that the therapeutic culture lacks Nietzsche's sense of the tragic nature of life.

The twentieth century has seen many attacks on Christianity, but the frontal attacks of militant atheists, Marxists and Nazis have not resulted in so much lost ground for Christians as the more insidious attacks of the therapeutic culture. The sense of guilt, the sense of sin, the sense of the sacred, the sense that there is another order of authority by which we are judged – these have not disappeared entirely from Christian culture, but they have suffered a profound erosion. If this is difficult to see, it's because of the fog which the culture of therapy emits – an empathic fog which surrounds us and confuses us and prevents us from seeing life clearly. We wander around in this fog thinking our enemy is our friend because he is so exquisitely concerned with our health.

The only thing that is powerful enough to cut through this fog is the light of revelation. Part of that revelation reminds us that physical and emotional health is not the be-all and end-all of existence. The most startling reminder is in the Gospel of Mark where we are told that if our hand offends us we should cut it off, it being better to enter into life maimed, than having two hands to go into hell. Likewise, it may be better to enter the kingdom of Heaven with a repressed psyche than to enter the other place brimming with self-assertiveness. We might also remind ourselves that there is no ultimate consolation in the theories propounded by psychologists. Psychology has very little to say to the majority of suffering people in this world, and absolutely nothing to say to the fact that all of us must one day die. Let us not sell our heritage for a mess of psychological pottage. And let us remember that there are far greater visions in Christianity than the vision of the whole person.

SOCIALIZATION: A THEOLOGICAL PERSPECTIVE

Cynthia Toolin

For a starting point, we can say that when human infants are born they are entirely helpless. They depend entirely on others for their survival, and in childhood they continue to depend on others for their survival and for their physical, psychological, spiritual, and social development. They continue in this dependence over an extended period of years. Infants and young children have no ability to socially function in their society; only after many years, do they socially function well. One of the most significant phenomena sociologists have studied is the process by which infants slowly mature into socially functioning members of society.

Although everyone agrees that this process occurs, different explanations of how it occurs have been offered over time. I think these explanations are of interest to theologians because we know that it is our nature to be social. As social beings we need to live in a society, in fact, we must live in society from our earliest years if we are to survive and if we are to develop properly and fulfill our potential. We want to understand this process because God has created us as social beings, and, as the Catechism of the Catholic Church says, there is a "resemblance between the unity of the divine persons and the fraternity that men are to establish among themselves in truth and love."[1] These explanations are of interest, then, because of the social nature God

[1] *Catechism of the Catholic Church* (New York: Catholic Book Publishing Co., 1994), #1878.

has given us and because at some level there is a resemblance between the internal live of the Trinity and the social life of men.

The explanations of this process can be classified under the broad headings of nature, the things we inherit biologically; nurture, the things we are taught in social interactions; or nature and nurture in some combination.[2]

Nature, Nurture, or Both

Nature

The argument that infants and children slowly mature into socially functioning members of society due to nature is based on the fact that humans are animals. As such, it is clear that we share much with other animals – for example, birth, death, the ingestion and elimination of nutrients, and some might argue, instincts. Instincts can be defined as biologically inherited ways of performing complex behavior. They are often evidenced in the animal kingdom; examples include the migratory patterns of some birds and insects, and the communal life of bees and ants. Instincts are specific to species (e.g., birds and insects do not share the same instincts). Both may have a migratory instinct, but it differs in when and how they migrate, as well as in their destinations. Instincts are also possessed by each appropriate member of the species (e.g., queen bees and worker bees do not possess the same instincts).

If humans have instincts, as strictly defined (i.e., biologically inherited ways of performing complex behavior), they are not apparent. Humans can not perform complex

[2] Most of the studies cited are classic ones, dating from 1940 to 1962. Studies of the socialization process occur frequently in the current sociological literature, refining, making distinctions, and adding nuances to earlier studies. Older studies are used here to emphasize generally accepted explanations that have withstood the test of time (i.e., to emphasize those things we have known, if only in a rudimentary way, for decades.)

tasks until they are taught how to do them. Different humans learn how to do the same complex tasks in various ways – e.g., by researching and reading about it, or by follow another's example. Humans exhibit a wide range of ability in performing complex tasks after they are learned. And lastly, if humans could perform complex tasks by instinct, the tasks would be performed in an identical (or nearly identical) manner in all societies. These four qualifications concerning how humans perform complex tasks show that humans do not have instincts, as strictly defined.

One example of a complex task is providing food for a family. Depending on which society a human lives in, provision of food can range from hunting, gathering, fishing, farming, going to the grocery store, going to a restaurant, or some combination of these options. Additional complexity can be seen by what technology is used in harvesting the food, by examining what plant or animal life is considered appropriate as food, how the food is prepared, and when, where, and how the food is consumed. Providing food is a complex task that must be learned in a specific society. This is a much different process than for an animal with a hunting instinct (e.g., a cat waiting by a rodent's burrow for its next meal to appear).

As Elkin and Handel said:[3]

> Lower forms of life – animals, birds, and insects – often function well merely by following inborn patterns of goal-directed activity that have persisted relatively unchanged for thousands of years. No comparable built in mechanisms exist in human beings, and in order to function within society, we must learn from others:

So an argument of biological determinism, that is, that infants and children mature into socially functioning members of society as a result of nature alone, is clearly flawed.

---

[3] Frederick Elkin and Gerald Handel, *The Child and Society: The Process of Socialization*, 4th ed. (New York: Random House, 1984), p. 16.

Nurture

The argument that infants and children become socially functioning members of society due to nurture is based on the apparent variety of human societies and on studies of humans and other primates in early non-nurturing situations.

Nurture: Variety

The variety that exists among human societies, both geographically and historically, is truly astounding. The society into which human infants and children are born affects their later social functioning. This is so apparent it needs little explanation. For instance, the language and customs of children are the language and customs of the society into which they are born. Children born in Argentina do not grow up speaking Swahili or behaving like Chinese. Humans learn these things, like language and culture, as they are nurtured by their parents or by parental substitutes (e.g., largely family and school), and as they are taught by nonparental influences (e.g., peer groups and mass media) in a particular society.

Nurture: Human Non-Nurturing Situations

Studies of humans and other primates in early non-nurturing situations are also of interest for understanding how infants and children become socially functioning members of society. It is generally believed that the early nurturing a child receives determines to a large extent the social functioning of that child when he becomes an adult. We see this belief in the popular culture. When a mass murderer is apprehended, the first thing people want to know about is his childhood. It is possible to draw some conclusions about the accuracy of this belief by longitudinally studying the effects of early non-nurturing situations.

While it would clearly be immoral to deliberately subject human infants and children to early non-nurturing situations, there are, unfortunately, examples of this occurring frequently in society. Studies that deal with the social isolation of children, and of "wild" or "feral" children, document these examples.

Classic studies by Kingsley Davis[4] showed the effects of social isolation on two illegitimate daughters of two mothers. Davis first documented the case of Anna, the second illegitimate child of her mother. She was discovered at age 6, confined in a small chair in a dark room, where she had been incarcerated for most of her life and where she had had a bare minimum of social contact. When she was discovered she could not eat by herself, clean herself, control her waste functions, walk, or talk; she apparently had no intellectual capacity.

After several years in various county homes, and just prior to her death at age 10, she could feed and clean herself, walk, play, and control her waste functions. She could talk mainly in phrases. Her social development was evidenced in that she tried to hold conversations with others and in that she loved a doll. These two show that she was developing socially. Davis thought that her isolation had prevented much later intellectual development, although the possibility also exists that she was congenitally feeble minded.

Davis then documented the case of Isabelle. Isabelle, who was discovered at age 6 in seclusion, was the illegitimate daughter of a deaf-mute woman. She was able to communicate with her mother by means of gestures. After she was found she was placed in a rigorous training program. The program was very successful, and she went through the stages of learning common to those aged 1 to 6 in a rapid, and proper succession. By age 14 she had passed the sixth grade in a public school and socialized with other children.

Davis compared the two girls – both were found at a

Kingsley Davis, "Extreme Social Isolation of a Child," *American Journal of Sociology* 45 (1940), pp. 554–65; "Final Note on a Case of Extreme Isolation," *American Journal of Sociology* 52 (1947), pp. 432–37.

very low intellectual level, both were initially considered to be congenitally feeble minded, and both attained a higher intellectual level. However, Anna remained at a somewhat low level after over four years, while Isabelle was almost normal in two years. The explanation may be that there was a different native intellectual capacity between the two girls. Davis, however, believed it was probably because Isabelle received more dedicated and intensive training. I would suggest the difference might also have been caused by the fact that Isabelle could communicate with her mother on some level, while Anna was ignored and rejected.

Other studies report on "wild" children (children found in the wild who survived for some time without adult care) and on "feral" children (children probably abandoned in the wild when they were old enough to have developed some survival skills but were reputed to have been brought up by wild animals). The conclusions of these case studies are of interest.

The story of Victor, the most famous of these children, was documented in Itard's[5] case study. Victor, an 11 or 12 year old boy, was captured by three hunters in the Caune woods in southern France in September 1799. He was brought to Paris the following year. People flocked to see the "Wild Boy of Aveyron" in hopes of seeing a primitive human. Rousseau had romanticized primitive humanity, uncorrupted by the influences of civilization, as the noble savage. The people of Paris were disappointed; instead of seeing the noble savage they expected to see, they saw a

> disgustingly dirty child affected with spasmodic movements and often convulsions who swayed back and forth ceaselessly like certain animals in the menagerie, who bit and scratched those who opposed him, who showed no sort of affection for those who attended him; and who was in short, indifferent to everything and attentive to nothing.[6]

[5] Jean-Marc-Gaspard Itard, *The Wild Boy of Aveyron* (Englewood Cliffs, NJ: Prentice Hall, 1962).

[6] Itard, p. 4.

Doctor Itard thought he could help Victor. He estimated that Victor had been left for dead, after having had his throat slit, at age 4 or 5. Because he had not been with other humans for many years, he had forgotten everything he had been taught in his early years. Accordingly, Itard described him as "much less an adolescent imbecile than a child or ten or twelve moths, and a child who would have the disadvantages of anti-social habits, a stubborn inattention, organs lacking in flexibility and a sensibility accidentally dulled."[7]

After two years, Doctor Itard had helped Victor considerably. He was "'an almost normal child who could not speak' but lived like a human being; clean affectionate, even able to read a few words and to understand much that was said to him." In a report made to the Minister of the Interior in 1806, Doctor Itard assessed Victor's progress, especially concerning his intellectual faculties. He believed that Victor's education was not complete and probably never would be. He concluded children were able to learn quickly from the civilization that surrounded them, but that Victor had been deprived of those surroundings for too long to ever develop fully.[8]

Clearly, abandoned children like Victor do not have the wonderfully full lives of the mythological feral children, Romulus and Remus, who were believed to have founded Rome.

Nurture: Primate Non-Nurturing Situations

Other studies have examined the effects of early non-nurturing situations on other primates. Conclusions of this kind of study, such as Harry Harlow's[9] classic ones on the

[7] Itard, p. 10.

[8] Itard, p. 100.

[9] See, for example, Harry Harlow and Robert Zimmerman, "Affectional Responses in the Infant Monkey," *Science* 21 (1959), pp. 421–32; Harry Harlow and Margaret Harlow, "Social Deprivation in Monkeys," *Scientific American* 207 (1962), pp. 137–46.

effects of social isolation on newborn monkeys, can be only cautiously generalized to humans. There is a qualitative difference between humans and other primates that must never be forgotten. Pope Pius XII, in his encyclical *Humani Generis*, spoke about discussions between positive scientists and theologians concerning the doctrine of evolution. He said that the Church does not forbid these discussions as long as men of faith remember that the Church obliges them "to hold that souls are immediately created by God."[10] That is, that if man did evolve from other human-like species, there is a qualitative difference based on God's creation of the soul.

There is also a quantitative difference present. Harlow and Zimmerman, although not speaking of the soul, made the point that

> the use of laboratory animals has serious limitations, for most of these animals have behavioral repertoires very different from those of the human being, and in many species these systems mature so rapidly that it is difficult to measure and assess their orderly development.[11]

On the other hand, subhuman primates

> are born at a state of maturity which makes it possible to begin precise measurements within the first few days of life. Furthermore, their postnatal maturation rate is slow enough to permit precise assessment of affectional variables and development.[12]

Thus, the results of these studies are still of interest as indicating the effects of non-nurturing situations in a species similar to *homo sapiens*.

[10] Pope Pius XII, *Humani Generis* (Boston, MA: Daughters of St. Paul, 1950), #36.

[11] Harlow and Zimmerman, p. 421.

[12] Harlow and Zimmerman, p. 421.

Harlow and his associates discovered that the social isolation of newborn monkeys resulted in the later presence of
emotional problems. He and his colleagues had intended to
establish a disease-free colony of monkeys for scientific
research. To do so, newborn monkeys were removed from
their mothers within a few hours of birth and kept in a con-
trolled environment. More separated newborns survived
and were healthy than those who remained with their
mothers; unfortunately, they were later discovered to also
be emotionally disturbed. Those who were raised in isolation *never* developed normal, social, emotional, sexual, or
maternal behavior (e.g., mothers would ignore, reject or kill
their newborns). The seriousness of the maladjustment var-
ied with the amount of time in isolation.

Upon making these discoveries, Harlow and his colleagues conducted a series of experiments in which newborn monkeys were offered a surrogate mother – one was
made of a bare wire frame, the other of a wire frame covered with terry cloth. The newborn monkeys preferred the
terry cloth covered surrogate under a variety of feeding
and fear inducing situations; they also formed a strong and
lasting attachment to the terry cloth covered surrogate.
Harlow and Harlow interpreted this as indicating a strong
biological need for closeness and comfort, and for social
contact, in the early period of life. They said:[13]

> Our first few experiments in the total isolation of these
> animals would thus appear to have bracketed what
> may be the critical period of development during
> which social experience is necessary for normal
> behavior in later life. . . . The indications are that six
> months of isolation will render the animals perma-
> nently inadequate. Since the rhesus monkey is more
> mature than the human infant at birth and grows four
> times more rapidly, this is equivalent to two or three
> years for the human child. On the other hand, there is
> reason to believe that the effects of shorter periods of

[13] Harlow and Harlow, pp. 143–44.

early isolation, perhaps 60 to 90 days or even more, are clearly reversible. This would be equivalent to about six months in the development of the human infant. The time probably varies with the individual and with the experiences to which it is exposed once it is removed from isolation. Beyond a brief period of neonatal grace, however, the evidence suggests that every additional week or month of social deprivation increasingly imperils social development in the rhesus monkey. Case studies of children reared in impersonal institutions or in homes with indifferent mothers or nurses show a frightening comparability. The child may remain relatively unharmed through the first months of life. But from this time on the damage is progressive and cumulative. By one year of age he may sustain enduring emotional scars and by two years many children have reached the point of no return.

So an argument of nurturing only, that is, that infants and children mature into socially functioning members of society as a result of nurture alone, has quite a bit of support in studies that show the social non-functioning of adult humans and primates who are deprived of early nurturing. When early nurturing does not occur, as these studies show, normal social functioning is difficult if not impossible to attain.

Note that Harlow and his associates were focusing on nurture in their studies, not nature. Yet, Harlow and Harlow stated that the need for closeness and comfort, for social contact, seemed to be biological. That is, the need for nurturing, without which normal development seems to be impossible, is based in nature.

Nature and Nurture

Today most sociologists would probably agree that adult social functioning is impacted by both nature and nurture.[14]

[14] As Humphrey said (Itard, *The Wild Boy*, xiv): Now the physical and mental structure of all human beings, feeble-minded and normal alike, develops through the play of hereditary and

Sociologists know that humans are not just social beings, but also biological ones. Accordingly, both social and biological factors, and the relationship between the two, must be addressed in order to understand social functioning. Nature sets human limitations on social functioning – e.g., intellectual capacity, race, sex, genetically caused physical or mental handicaps, etc.; nurture defines the meaning of these limitations for social functioning. I would argue that the more important of the two is nurture. Consider the social functioning of a brilliant black woman if she was a slave in rural Mississippi in the 1850s, an unwed welfare mother in a small town in Massachusetts in the 1960s, or a senior partner of a major law firm in New York City in the 1990s. Her social functioning would not be the same in all three situations. In this example, nature is responsible for the intellectual capacity, race and sex of the person; nurture is responsible for the social functioning of the person by determining the meaning of the intellectual capacity, race, and sex in the three different societies.

Socialization

The nurturing process by which an infant or child becomes a socially functioning member of society is call

environmental conditions. After the fertilization of the ovum, every particle of matter in the human organism is contributed from the environment, the interaction of specific environmental conditions with a fertilized ovum of a definite character determining the nature of the resulting structure. Environmental influences begin before birth and continue after birth as general environment, both physiological and social; those environmental influences that are deliberately and systematically applied we call formal education. Itard's original mistake was apparently to assume, as the result of a somewhat amateurish philosophy, that environment could accomplish everything; that a boy who was not a normal human being could necessarily be made normal by the proper training. He failed to see that, even though he had been correct in this supposition, the environmental corrective must be applied at the right time. Training may clearly be too late – or too early.

socialization. I would define it as the lifelong process[15] by which humans learn to participate in social groups and in a society, learning the various skills that are defined as necessary by its culture (e.g., social or intellectual skills).

Thomas Gilby, O.P., in discussing *Summa Theologiae* I, 1, 6, 2, explained how theology can judge other sciences both positively, "by interpreting them in the light of God's dealing with men," and negatively, "by correcting inferences that may be drawn from them."[16] It would seem that on this basis sociological explanations of behavior can also be judged. As theologians, then, we can examine the understanding of the socialization process and critique inferences that can be drawn from it, both positively and negatively.

Positive Critique

From these studies focused on the lack of nurturing of human and primate infants and children, it is clear that both infants and children must have close comforting contact with parents (or parental substitutes) in order to develop into socially functioning adults.

As theologians we can clearly support the inferences that can be drawn from these findings. The family is ordered not only to the good of the two spouses, but also to the procreation and education of children. It is the social unit of primary importance to people of all ages, but particularly to children. To socialize infants and children, to move them from biological humans to socially functioning humans, requires a close, comforting, stable nurturing relationship such as can only be provided in the family. Parents teach their children by words and deeds,[17] by what they say and

[15] Socialization is a life long process. Adults are socialized every time they change a status (e.g., from employed to retired, from married to widowed.) For adults it is usually a more conscious and deliberate process than for children.

[16] Thomas Gilby, O.P., ed., *Summa Theologiae*, Blackfriars, vol. 1 (New York: McGraw-Hill Book Company, 1964), pp. 22–23.

[17] An early sociologist, Charles Horton Cooley, thought humans develop through what is called the "looking glass"

by the example of their lives. They teach them the skills they need to live in this life. By word and by example, they teach them how to interact with themselves, with their siblings, with other family members, and eventually with people outside the family. Hopefully, although I am not sure of how often this happens, parents will teach their children the proper attitude towards the things of this life in light of our ultimate end (i.e., a true hierarchy of value, not an inverted one) and about the meaning of human life.

process. In this process, humans first imagine how they appear to others in a particular situation. Second, they imagine how others will react to that appearance. Lastly, humans modify themselves according to these imagined perceptions. For example, a new manager about to start his first day at the office imagines how others will see him as he carefully chooses his clothes. As he puts on a starched white shirt, black bow tie, gray suit with cuffs, and black shoes he imagines his new staff will see him as conservative and intelligent. He imagines they will react to him as a decisive man with true power and authority, a natural born leader. If he likes these imagined perceptions, he will wear the outfit; if he doesn't like them, he will wear a different one.

The looking glass process is an evaluation of the imagined perceptions of others. This evaluation ranges from being accurate to being notoriously inaccurate. The new manager in the example could be correct – his staff could see him as exhibiting all these qualities he imagined; he could also be incorrect – his staff could see him as a man with bad taste in clothes, or as hopelessly outdated, or as too conservative. Regardless of the accuracy of inaccuracy of the imagination, the result will be the same because the person imagining thinks he is correct.

As humans pass through life, the imagined perceptions and reactions of others are not equally important. George Herbert Mead, a sociologist who built on the work of Cooley, pointed out that the judgements of some people are more important. These people – he called them significant others – vary as time passes. In childhood, immediate family members and teachers are probably the most important; in adolescence, members of peer groups are more important in many matters, while family members and teachers are more important in others; in adulthood, the spouse is probably the most important.

In the family the biological human is born and the social human is developed. The family is absolutely necessary to the development of infants and children, physically, intellectually, socially, and most importantly, spiritually.[18] The Catechism rightly says that "family life is an initiation into life in society."[19]

Negative Critique

One negative criticism of the understanding of the process of socialization centers on the problems of inexact terminology. It is true that infants and young children do not know how to function in a particular society. They do not, for instance know how to speak in a grammatically correct manner, eat at a table using appropriate utensils, practice good hygiene, or even control bodily waste functions. Years pass while parents, parental substitutes, and others teach the child these behaviors, all of which are considered characteristically human. When sociologists use the term socialization to refer to the process whereby an infant or child is taught these characteristically human behaviors, the term is correctly used. However, there is an inexactness involved when the term is used either to state or to imply that the infant or child *becomes* human during the socialization process.

In discussing Anna's slow progress, Davis said:[20]

> A month later more improvement along the same lines was noted. Though grave limitations remained, Anna was definitely becoming more of a human being.

Developmentalism

Using the term in this way leads to the serious error of developmentalism. By developmentalism I mean the belief

---

[18] One of the most important is to help children find their vocation, and then to support them in that choice.

[19] *Catechism of the Catholic Church*, #2207.

[20] Davis, "Extreme Social Isolation," p. 561.

that as time passes, an infant or a child is in the process of becoming human; that there is a time when a genetically human being becomes more human, leaving behind a stage that was less human.[21] Examples of a developmental belief can be seen in the popular pro-abortion bumper sticker, "It's a choice, not a child" and in support given to the legality of partial birth abortion. In both cases, the unborn are not seen as humans, or as fully human, or as humans of worth. Being human is not something an infant or child develops into; it is what they are. The infant or the child is not something else (e.g., subhuman, prehuman, extra human, inhuman) and them human. No mater where the infant or child is in the socialization process, he or she is always a human infant or a human child.

The sociologist Steven Nock made an important distinction between the biological human and the social human. He pointed out that everyone is a biological human. He believed biological humans become social humans through the process of socialization. (Actually humans are social beings by nature; in the socialization process humans learn how to function as the social beings they already are.) Yet, even though he had a fairly clear understanding of everyone being human, Nock wen on to say[22] "without regular contact with other humans, an individual will be become what we consider to be a human person."

I believe the only way in which the socialization process can be appropriately understood is that all are both biological humans and social beings. But to perform the behaviors that are thought of as characteristically human, that is, to be socially functioning humans, infants and children must be

[21] This make no sense as the genetics of a new member of a species is set at the time of conception. As soon as the chromosomes "join," a new life of that species is begun – there is nothing else it is, nor anything else it will be, than a new member of that species.

[22] Steven Nock, *Sociology of the Family* (Englewood Cliffs, NJ: Prentice Hall, 1992), p. 217.

taught behavior appropriate to their society during the socialization process.

Consequences of Terminology

Terminology is very important, because when it is used in an inexact manner, the consequences can be dire. An inexact meaning of the term socialization can lead to two negative consequences: it can lead to only some biological humans being defined as being truly human and it can lead to a misunderstanding of the value and dignity of each human life. If people are defined as not human, or as humans of lesser value or dignity, the worse consequence that can follow is the withholding of human rights. In the culture of death present in much of the world today we already see this consequence and we must fight it.

If we define as human only those who can perform characteristically human behaviors, those who cannot or do not or will not perform them are, by definition, no human. Eating at a table using the appropriate utensils is considered a characteristically human behavior in the United States. People who do not yet know how to do this (infants, young children), who have forgotten how to do this (the senile), who cannot do this (the physically handicapped), who are in a state which precludes doing this (those is a coma), or who do this in a different manner (those using chop sticks) could be defined as being not human because they do not exhibit behavior defined as characteristically human. This example may seem extreme – after all, who would define someone as not human because they cannot, do not, or will not eat at a table? I, however, do not think the example is an extreme as being defined as not human because of physical location inside the womb, instead of outside it. This happens everyday in the United States, even to late term fetuses.

Even if humans who cannot, do not, or will not perform characteristically human behaviors are defined appropriately as human, they may be defined as humans of lesser value or dignity than those who can, or do, or will perform such behaviors. The resultant problem is that to be considered a human of worth, one would have to be human plus something else. For instance the argument could be made that to be of worth a human must be genetically human and regularly eat at a table. The example again seems extreme – who would say a human is not of worth on the basis of not regularly eating at a table? Again, I do not think the example is as extreme as being defined as a human of lesser worth because of being genetically human, but not viable outside the womb. This happens every day in the United States to early term fetuses.[23]

Obligations of Theologians

As theologians we are obligated to give witness to the truth, to defend it, to explain it, and to share it. Accordingly, as theologians we must emphasize that all are touched by God, and that all are human from the moment of conception. The Catechism states "every spiritual soul is created immediately by God – it is not 'produced' by the parents – and also that it is immortal."[24] We must emphasize that all

---

[23] There is another reason that it is important for theologians to understand the concept of socialization. Young adults in sociology classes in colleges and universities all over the world have been taught this concept for decades. To receive a passing grade in a sociology course, or to go on to advanced studies or work in the sociological field, it is necessary to have an adequate understanding of this basic foundational concept.

When the concept is used in classrooms and textbooks properly, that is, to explain how biological humans learn to become socially functioning humans, the terminology is correctly used. The problem is that sometimes it is used inexactly, implying or stating that we become human in the process of socialization. Students leave classes with an erroneous understanding of what it means to be human, and correspondingly of the value and dignity of each human life. This wrong understanding reinforces, and is reinforced by, popular erroneous views in society of the meaning of human life, and of its value and dignity, especially as defined by quality of life.

are humans of equal worth even when they cannot, do not, or will not perform characteristically human things. All humans have the same origin, God, who created man in him image. All humans have the same redemption, through the life, passion, death and resurrection of Christ. All humans have the same ultimate end, or destiny, of eternal communion with God. It does not matter if a human is old and crippled, young and retarded, middle aged and healthy, or unborn – all are fully human, all are of equal value, and all are of equal dignity. We are obligated to give witness to this truth in the way we live our lives, in the way we fulfill our vocations, and in the way we practice our science.[25]

Conclusion

Harlow and Harlow's conclusions that, first, without early nurturing (in primates) later normal social functioning is impossible, and second, that there seems to be a need

[24] *Catechism of the Catholic Church*, #366.

[25] We can also show the results of the human's need for one another. The Catechism says (#1936–37): On coming into the world, man in not equipped with everything he needs for developing his bodily and spiritual life. He needs others. Differences appear tied to age, physical abilities, intellectual or moral aptitudes. . . . These differences belong to God's plan, who wills that each receive what he needs from others, and that those endowed with particular 'talents' share the benefits with those who need them.

All humans need others. While some use these inequalities and inabilities as the basis for defining others as being not human or as being humans of lesser value or dignity, we theologians can point to the wonderful opportunities presented by these differences. The opportunities to help others aid in converting this world into the kingdom of God, and results in spiritual and moral growth for those who take advantage of these situations. The Catechism goes on to say (#1937), "these differences encourage and often oblige persons to practice generosity, kindness, and sharing of goods."

for closeness and comfort, or nurture, rooted in nature, are very important. God created humans as social beings; he put a need for others in our nature that is so crucial we cannot survive or develop normally without its satisfaction.

God created the first society, Adam and Even, one of each sex, male and female. This first society, marriage, was ordered to the good of the spouses (i.e., to nurture each other) and to the procreation and education of children (i.e., to cooperate with God in bringing hew humans into the world and then to nurture them). Marriage is still ordered the same way.

The need, rooted in nature, for closeness and comfort, for social contact, can be satisfied adequately only in a loving, stable nurturing process of socialization in a family. That is the way God planned it.

SCIENCE, FAITH, AND ATHEISM

Don DeMarco

"Science is agnosticism," proclaimed Thomas Huxley. it is a richly ambiguous remark. The word "agnosticism," we must remember, has no inherent reference to the Deity. It fundamentally refers to a person's state of "not knowing" or even "knowing nothing." In this sense, Huxley's statement is false. Science does, indeed, provide us with real knowledge. In another sense of the term, agnosticism is traditionally linked with an absence of knowledge concerning the existence of God. But even in this sense, the statement is equally untenable because the knowledge gained through science, far from drawing a blank with regard to the reality of God, actually furnishes us with an intellectual bridge to His existence.

Dr. Werner von Braun, the "Father of the Saturn 5 Rocket" that made it possible for 12 men to walk on the surface of the moon, is one of innumerable scientists who do not think that science precludes knowledge of God. As a scientist, and surely an eminent one, he states that "Anything as well ordered and perfectly created as is our earth and universe must have a Maker, a Master Designer. Anything so orderly, so perfect, so precisely balanced, so majestic as this creation can only be the product of a Divine Idea." The existence of order presupposes a designer, just as the existence of a law presupposes a legislator.

Reason, including scientific reason, moves easily and naturally from effect to Cause, discovering in the-natural order implications for the existence of a higher order. Christians, surely, should have no fear that reason and science lead to an agnosticism of God. As St. Paul has written, "Test all things; hold fast to that which is good" (1Th 5.21). For Paul, God and man, faith and reason, life and love, are marvelously unified in Christ: Christ dwells in the intellect by faith, in the heart and affections by charity, and in the soul by grace.

If science does not lead to agnosticism, even less can it lead to atheism. Pope John Paul II states in his international best-seller, *Crossing the Threshold of Hope*, that the visible world, in and of itself, cannot offer a scientific basis for an atheistic interpretation of reality. Consequently, an atheistic interpretation would be "one-sided and tendentious." He then goes on to recall participating in many meetings with scientists, in particular, with physicists, who, after Einstein, were quite open to a theistic interpretation of the world.

The dictum "Science is agnosticism," then, is not particularly rational; rather, it is the proclamation of a credo. It does not oppose, but actually presupposes faith, the gratuitous belief that science and faith will prove to be incompatible with each other. Let us read more from the thought of von Braun: "There are those who say that science and religion are incompatible. Nothing could be further from the truth. Science seeks to answer the questions about creation, and religion seeks to learn about the Creator." Science and faith are convergent, not divergent. Just as the creative act of the Creator and His creation are in continuity with each other, so, too, though in reverse order, are the scientific inquiry that illuminates creation and the reasonable faith in the Divine Being that the findings of such scientific inquiry imply.

"Science is agnosticism," therefore, is not a paradox. Nor is it an oxy-moron. It is simply a contradiction. Nonetheless, the myth persists that science and faith, reason and religion, are mutually exclusive.

Allow me to offer a personal example that may help bring into focus the contradiction involved in making the activity of reason (or science that is based on reason) incompatible with faith in God.

I recently had an article published in the secular press in which I made the point in passing that the ultimate source of all authority is God. What I thought to be a non-inflammatory remark nonetheless inflamed a local atheist who dispatched an angry letter to me. Before opening the envelope, that bore an address I did not recognize, I noticed the words: "Nothing Fails Like Prayer!" thoughts immediately turned to a recent conference on cancer held in Kingston, Ontario at which one of the participating scientists stated to the Media that the only factor we can be sure about that benefits cancer patients in the recovery of their health is prayer. And she had the statistical data to back her claim. I thought it rather curious that someone would use envelopes to beseech the world not to pray. It is like urging others to become solipsists. What is pre-supposed by the philosophy is negated by its very expression.

I read the letter and was informed that I was guilty of "making irrelevant and spurious character assaults" against all atheists. My atheist advisor informed me that if I contend that God is the source of authority, I logically implied that those who do not believe in God have no basis for their authority, and consequently are immoral.

While this is an interesting point, it is entirely bereft of logic. Imagine, for example, a young desert-dweller who has never seen rain. He knows about water, which he uses on a daily basis. But he believes, due to his limited experience, that the ultimate source of water is the local oasis. He knows about water, but is understandably mistaken about its ultimate source. To see it rain for the first time would be a wonder and revelation to him. Similarly, it is possible to know about morality and even be highly moral, without knowing that God is the ultimate source of morality. An atheist can manifest attributes of God – love, kindness, generosity – without knowing that God is the ultimate source of these virtues, just as easily as a person can wear a particular hat while remaining ignorant of the identity of its milliner. Moral behavior is one thing, its foundation is quite another.

The letter was actually quite strong in its denunciation of me, accusing me of making the kind of "nonsensical" and "unsubstantiated claims" that "continue to do much damage in our society today." His underlying point, however, was really the contrary of what he expressed. He was implying (though perhaps without realizing it) that it is precisely the people who believe in God who are immoral because they establish their morality on a basis that does not exist and therefore cannot be truly moral. Of course, this makes no sense either, but it is curious that my atheist instructor can enjoy the liberty of advising the world not to pray, while denying anyone the liberty to assert that God is the source of all authority.

If God exists of course, the issue is settled. But our atheist does not want to deal with the question of God's existence. He simply assumes He does not. But he also assumes that the activity of human reason and the existence of God are disjunctive. Therefore, the only truly reasonable people in the world are atheists.

I have always found it odd that a person who neither believes in God, the supernatural, the immortality of the soul, the consolation of religion, and so on, could be apostolic about such barrenness. It would be like discovering that your grandfather was a completely unscrupulous fellow and devoid of a single redeeming quality, and then sending letters out to complete strangers, informing them of this embarrassing and disconcerting fact. Is it that misery loves company? Or that certain people, like gossip columnists, love to spread bad news?

The debate that an apostolic atheist wages against faithful Christians is also a bit odd. He wants everyone to believe that his ancestry goes back to mud and slime, and holds that it is damaging to one's self-esteem to believe that a human being is made in the image of God.

But my atheist correspondent does not operate alone. He is a member of the Freedom From Religion Foundation. In keeping with his apostolic zeal, he sent me information about how and at what price. I could become a supporter of "freethought" and a subscriber to *Freethought Today* ("the only freethought newspaper in the United States").

My single and seemingly innocuous reference to the Deity precipitated a virtual attack by the one agency in the world that, presumably, would be the most likely one to leave me alone – the freethought brigade! Apparently, believing in God impairs my freedom, even if I freely came to the belief that God exists, and freely hold to it.

I opened one of the pamphlets that came with the letter ("Nontract No. 3" as it is called). I read the following passage: "We are all born atheists." A startling suggestion! But is it not premature to ascribe a theologico-philosophical position to the mind of a neonate? Was this a self-defeating admission that had eluded the writers of this statement, for in the newborn, ignorance is at its high point. Are we most free when we are most ignorant? Is it not the truth that will make us free, not ignorance of it? No one is born knowledgeable or virtuous; no one is born with the conviction that God does not exist. Atheism is not a natural endowment. A blank sheet of paper is unprinted, but it is not unimprintable.

More startling, two sentences later, however, was the assertion that among the great artists exemplifying the spirit of the sceptic or the freethinker who refused to bend to religion, is Alfred Lord Tennyson. This seemed to be a particularly bad example of a role model for irreligion. The most often quoted line from the pen of this great Victorian poet is a glowing testimony to the efficacy of prayer: "More things are wrought by prayer than this world dreams of."

I put the pamphlet aside and opened a critical edition of Tennyson's great poem, *In Memoriam*, and read the first stanza:

> Strong Son of God, immortal Love,
> Whom we, that have not seen thy face,
> By faith, and faith alone, embrace,
> Believing where we cannot prove.

Tennyson himself advised that the opening line "might be taken in a St. John sense": "In him was life, and the life was the light of men. The light shines in the darkness, and the darkness has not overcome it" (John 1,4-5).

This did not sound like the style of a freethinking atheist. Tennyson, in fact, had from boyhood a deep religious sense and a genuine capacity for mystical experience. Scholars have hailed *In Memoriam* as the most dramatic as well as the most religious of English elegies. Queen Victoria, upon losing her husband, stated that *In Memoriam* was her comfort, second only to the Bible.

In Memoriam, inspired by the sudden death (at age twenty-two) of Tennyson's dear and closest friend, Arthur Henry Hallam, charts the triumphal journey from doubt to faith. In Tennyson's mind, reason and faith were not antagonistic to each other in the least. This is amply evident in the following two stanzas from *In Memoriam's* "Prologue":

> We have but faith: we cannot know;
> For knowledge is of things we see;
> And yet we trust it comes from thee,
> A beam in darkness: let it grow.
>
> Let knowledge grow from more to more,
> But more of reverence in us dwell;
> That mind and soul, according well,
> May make one music as before,

Tennyson laments the modern world's loss of faith. "As before" refers to the age of faith that characterized the Middle Ages, before modern science had created the gulf between intellectual "knowledge," on the one hand, and instinctive "reverence" on the other. Reason and faith, knowledge and reverence, should harmonize to make one music.

Tennyson is hardly an apologist for the "freethinker." He is, by all accounts, a deeply religious Christian who knows the limitations of knowledge and the need or faith. He knows, all too well, that he is not free to reject either.

I proceeded to "Nontract No. ll," which purports to explain "What is a Freethinker?" Here I read that freethinkers are not entirely free but are bound by the natural order. They are "naturalistic." "Truth," the pamphlet goes on to state, "is the degree to which a statement corresponds with reality." This sounded remarkably similar to St. Thomas Aquinas' notion of truth: "The human intellect is measured by things so that man's thought is not true on its own account but is called true in virtue of its conformity with things" (*Summa Theologiae* II–II, 26, 1 ad 2.). Could Aquinas (as well as Tennyson) be an apologist for atheistic freethinkers? Then why has the Church canonized him?

A freethinker, then, does have restraints. He is neither an ignorant child nor a reckless and licentious adult. His thinking, if it is to be true, must conform to reality. A freethinker, then, since his thought is limited only by reality, can be religious, since faith also has reality as its object. Therefore, reason and faith are perfectly compatible, though distinguishable, because they are united by the same object, namely, reality. Shoes and socks are distinguishable, but hot incompatible. A person may wear shoes and socks, just shoes, or just socks. So, too, a person may have reason and faith, or emphasize one more than the other. Tennyson, Aquinas, and my atheist correspondent can all be freethinkers, by the very tenets established by the Freedom from Religion Foundation. So what is all the huff?

The tract goes on to claim a basis for morality that is independent of religion. It cites a certain Barbara Walker who states: "What is moral is simply what does not hurt others. Kindness . . . sums up everything." Yet, as St. Thomas Aquinas notes: "The greatest kindness one can render to any man consists in leading him from error to truth" (*In div. nom.* 4,4.). Kindness cannot sum up everything, because if it did, it would exclude a proper concern for truth. It is not kind to allow a person to wallow in error.

I then turned to "Nontract No. 4" for further illumina-
tion. There I read a statement attributed to Gloria Steinem
that was supposed to embarrass anyone who believes in
religion: "It's an incredible con job when you think, of it, to
believe something now in exchange for life after death.
Even corporations with all their reward systems don't try
to make it posthumous."

Ms. Steinem is being glib. But her rhetoric is without rec-
titude. First, she mistakes a "covenant" for an "exchange."
Religion is not a deal (pay now, reap the rewards later), but
a loving relationship with God who is the essence of love.
Nor is there an essential discontinuity – between this world
and the next. Our happiness in the next life is a consequence (more properly than a reward") of our love in this
life. Moreover, it is inaccurate to suggest that we are dead
in the next world. We are not "posthumous" in paradise,
but very much alive (more so than ever before). in addition,
corporations do make their reward systems posthumous.
This is the normal way in which a widow or widower
receives life insurance benefits once the spouse has died.

Not wanting to abandon reality, or the laws of logic, I
came to the conclusion that the material sent to be directly
from my atheist letter-writer, and indirectly from the
Freedom From Religion Foundation is highly confused. There
would be a lot less quarreling and invective in the world if
there were less confusion. We human beings, diverse as we
are, are more alike than we often realize. But we have a
strange proclivity to isolate elements that belong to a
greater whole and then launch an artificial war between
absolutized fragments. Even doubt and belief co-exist in
the same person. The religious person is not one who is free
of all doubts (because of his presumed "blind faith"). Nor
is the atheist free of all belief. I was heartened by the atheist's complimentary close: "Best regards" (it was in stark
contrast with the cynical maxim on the envelope).

Cardinal Ratzinger states in his introduction to

Christianity that "both the believer and the unbeliever share, each in his own way, doubt and belief, if they do not hide away from themselves and from the truth of their being. Neither can quite escape doubt or belief: for the one, faith is present against doubt, for the other through doubt and in the form of doubt." Therese of Lisieux horrified some of her sisters when they read these words in the saint's diary: "I am assailed by the worst temptations of atheism."

Science depends on faith far more than is generally assumed. The scientist must make an initial act of faith that the world to which he applies reason is one whose laws are both intelligible and consistent. He must believe, or else he would lose heart and fear that the laws of the universe are like the croquet game in Alice in Wonderland, where the rules of the game change from moment to moment by the arbitrary decree of the Queen. For this reason, Norbert Wiener" – "Father of Cybernetics," who received a Harvard Ph.D. in mathematics at 18, and later wrote a book, *God and Golem Inc.*, which won the National Book Award in 1964 – asserts that "Science is impossible without faith."

When Albert Einstein confessed that what was most incomprehensible for him was the fact that the universe is comprehensible, he was alluding to the same need for faith. The laws of the universe are a fit object for human reason, but the reality of this affinity between mind and world, itself a mystery, demands the scientist's faithful allegiance. *"Der Herr Gott ist raffiniert, aber boshaft ist Er nicht,"* he wrote ("God is subtle, but not malicious"). We need reason, for the mind to discover the laws of the universe, but we need a preliminary faith that these laws will not betray us. Reason without faith lacks the confidence necessary to exercise its own act.

In addition, many of the truths of science, from quarks to quazars, involve aspects of reality that, while affirmable, are nonetheless inconceivable. In this way, the human mind is disposed to affirm realities that are real but nonetheless beyond comprehension. Let us return one final time to the thought of Dr. von Braun:

> The electron is materially inconceivable, and yet it is so perfectly known through its effects that we use it to illuminate our cities, guide our airlines through the night skies, and take the most accurate measurements.

> What strange rationale makes some physicists accept the inconceivable elctron as real, while refusing to accept the reality of God on the ground that they cannot conceive Him?

AN UNSCIENTIFIC POST-SCRIPT ON CATHOLICISM IN AN AGE OF SCIENCE

Archbishop George Pell

1. Science and the Changing Value of Human Life

Three great women made the headlines last year. St. Teresa of Calcutta died having poured out her life in low tech care for the most needy and abandoned of our planet. Princess Diana of Wales died at the hands of more sophisticated science, that of high speed glamour and glitz, the motorcar and flash photography. And Dolly the Sheep was born.

Dolly got less coverage in the newspapers and magazines than the other two ladies, and much of it was undoubtedly hype and hysteria. But it also reflected the growing realization that we are at the beginning of a bio-medical revolution more significant than industrialization, nuclear power or the computer. Recent advances mean we are fast acquiring the power to modify and control not only the world around us, the world which humanity must inhabit, but also humanity itself, the when and how and what of people's lives and deaths and much in between. Some of these means are already in use or at hand; others will be in the near future. All this presents some very exciting new opportunities and some very difficult new challenges for the Catholic Church and Western society which is marked by a very adult science sadly all too often hitched to a rather childish ethic and spirituality.

The cloned sheep was not the first headline-grabber to hail from Edinburgh in Scotland. From there came the proposal a few years ago that brain-dead women might be utilized as surrogate mothers (they used the word 'incubators') for others who could not carry their own children, or did not want to do so (pre-natal nannies). The next creative proposal from technologists in that city was that eggs of aborted girls might be used of IVF programmes, so that the dead unborn children would be the genetic mothers of children created for other people. Perhaps Scots scientists should stick to perfecting malt whiskeys.

The Scots wanted to use their cloning technique to create some special animals for medical research; but meanwhile Australian IVF scientists have been cloning cattle (by a different method) for big profits on the open market. Both assured us that human cloning was not on their drawing board. But the world was far from confident. After all, Australia's leading cattle-cloner, Alan Trounson, is also that country's leading human IVF technician. At his hands and those of others like him, perhaps 100,000 test tube babies were born around the world since 1978. Children for the infertile sounds great, at least until you learn a little more about the intrinsic immorality of the processes used, the risks to those involved, the hundred of thousands of embryos killed in the past few years or left in limbo in frozen storage. But what about artificial insemination and surrogacy for 'gay' couples; pregnancies for octogenarians; taking sperm from recently deceased men so the widow can have child; men carrying babies; cloned human beings used for spare parts; animal-human hybrids; genetic tests for unborn children's sex, coloring, likely shape, longevity, athletic and other physical potential; more genetic tests (and perhaps abortion) for unborn children's part-genetic behavioral dispositions such as schizophrenia, substance dependency, depression, aggressiveness, homosexuality, religiosity . . .

At the other end, we may soon be able to extend life to 120 years or so for those who want to live for much longer here on earth; or offer a quick medical injection for those who are sick of it. Until then we can help people to live healthier lives, in greater comfort, though at some considerable cost. Further improvements can be expected, not only in life-extension and health-improvement, but in medically-delivered 'quality of life', such as cures of chronic conditions such as arthritis, sight and hearing problems, and various changes to body shape, color, texture and so on. Cindy Jackson, who runs London's thriving 'Cosmetic Surgery Network,' recently made headlines by writing up the nine years, 37 operations, and hundreds of thousands of dollars she has so far spent on having herself surgically remade in the image of the Barbie Doll. And the big field for the future will be the scientific control of human capacities such as strength, agility, reflexes, emotion, memory, imagination, desire, libido, aggression, thought, choice, speech and action. Heroin, anabolic steroids, Prozac, these are only the tip of the pharmacological iceberg of the future. The possibilities in bioscience are tremendous!

Yet as Pope John Paul has noted: "The development of science and technology, this splendid testimony of the human capacity for understanding and for perseverance, does not free humanity from the obligation to ask the ultimate religious questions. Rather, it spurs us on to face the most painful and decisive of struggles, those of the heart and of the moral conscience."[1]

In a series of encyclicals culminating in *Tertio Millennio Adveniente* Pope John Paul II has challenged the Church and humanity, on the eve of a new millennium, to take stock of where we are going: like the prophets of old crying out to Israel "look at how you treat the widows, the orphans, the refugees," like Leo XIII proposing in *Rerum novarum* that how workers are treated is the test of our whole economies, *so John Paul now points to abortion, euthanasia and the reproductive technologies–how we treat the youngest and the oldest, the most vulnerable of people – as the lit-*

---

[1] *Veritatis Splendor* 1.

mus test for your civilization at this turning point in our history.

> Humanity today offers us a truly alarming spectacle, if we consider not only how extensively attacks on life are spreading but also their unheard-of numerical proportion, and the fact that they receive widespread and powerful support. . . . The twentieth century will have been an era of massive attacks on life, an endless series of wars and a continual taking of innocent human life. . . . On the eve of the Third Millennium, the challenge facing us is an arduous one: only the concerted efforts of all those who believe in the value of life can prevent a setback of unforeseeable consequences for civilization.[2]

Greeting *Evangelium vitae* enthusiastically, Paul Johnson in *The Spectator* agreed with the Pope as to what is ultimately at issue: "Crueler things were done [during the totalitarian 20th century], on a larger scale, and with more devilish refinement, than ever before in the sad story of mankind. . . . Still, the totalitarian century is behind us." He then continues "But it is already evident what we shall have to fear. In our own century, we allowed vicious men to play with the state, and paid the penalty of 150 million done to death by state violence. In the 21st century, the risk is that we will allow men – and women too – to play with human life itself."[3]

Johnson agrees with John Paul that there is much more at stake here in the great controversies over biotechnology than is commonly appreciated: in one of the most memorable phrases of his pontificate, the Pope declares that humanity at the turn of the millennium is in the midst of a dramatic conflict between the "culture of death" and the "culture of life."[4] And he pulls no punches as to its causes, both outside and inside the church: a wrong notion of free-

[2] *Evangelium Vitae* 17, 91.

[3] *The Spectator* (April 4, 1995), p. 22.

[4] *Evangelium vitae* 50.

dom, the "eclipse of the sense of God," a radical under-valuing of human life, all contributing to a "a social and cultural climate dominated by secularism."[5] This practical atheism has its impact upon science as elsewhere:

> Once all reference to God has been removed, it is not surprising that the meaning of everything else becomes profoundly distorted. Nature itself, from being *mater*, and is subjected to every kind of manipulation. This is the direction in which a certain technical and scientific way of thinking, prevalent in present-day culture, appears to be leading when it rejects the very idea that there is a truth of creation which must be acknowledged, or a plan of God for life which must be respected. . . . By living *as if God did not exist*, man not only loses sight of the mystery of God, but also of the mystery of the world and the mystery of his own being.[6]

Amidst his critique of the hidden violence in supposed-ly peaceful modern societies, the Pop acknowledges the contribution science, where there is, so much that is positive for the unborn, the suffering and those in an acute or terminal stage of sickness."[7] Science also allows couples to exercise responsible parenthood through advances in natural family planning.[8] And various agencies are making the benefits of advanced medicine available also in the developing countries; a considerable blessing.

On the other hand, in a society in which violence against the youngest and the oldest is increasingly condoned, the wonderful "new prospects opened up by scientific and technological progress" are turned into "new forms of attacks on the dignity of the human being."[9] Far from supporting the weak, scientific research in fertility and embry-

[5] *Ibid.*, 21.

[6] *Ibid.*, 22–23.

[7] *Ibid.*, 26.

[8] *Ibid.*, 97.

[9] *Ibid.*, 4.

ology becomes "almost exclusively preoccupied with developing products which are ever more simple and effective in suppressing life."[10]

> The various *techniques of artificial reproduction*, which would seem to be at the service of life and which are frequently used with this intention, actually open the door to new threats against life. Apart from the fact that they are morally unacceptable, since they separate procreation from the fully human context of the conjugal act, these techniques . . . expose human embryos to very great risks of death . . . embryos are over-produced . . . and [subsequently] destroyed or used for research which, under the pretext of scientific or medical progress, in fact reduces human life to the level of simple 'biological material' to be freely disposed of.

So prenatal testing, instead of being for diagnosis and treatment, all too often becomes a tool for "eugenic abortion," and handicapped babies even after birth are increasingly at risk. "In this way, we revert to a state of barbarism which one hoped had been left behind forever."[11]

Christ's Gospel of Life proposes an alternative to this reversion to neo-paganism. "Human life, as a gift of God ,is sacred and inviolable. The meaning of life is found in giving and receiving love, and in this light human sexuality and procreation reach their true and full significance. Love also gives meaning to suffering and death; despite the mystery which surrounds them, they can become saving events. *Respect for life requires that science and technology should always be at the serivce of man and his integral development.*"[12]

Science needs more than big grants, big labs, big kudos: as its power and potential for both good and ill grow exponentially every minute, it more desperately than ever needs

[10] *Ibid.*, 13.
[11] *Ibid.*, 14.
[12] *Ibid.*, 81.

moral wisdom, and democratic constraints. If we are to be improved and remade by science, Barbie should not be the model.

2. The Eclipse of the Sense of God

The scientific developments I have outlined make quite clear that this human remaking is not to be constrained to the realm of the body. The aspiration seems to be for the *total* remaking of man, to alter not only the individual's personality and character but – is such a thing were possible – his soul. We have noted that prenatal testing and abortion are already used eugenically to prevent the birth of children who are in any minor way "defective"; bearers of the genes for diseases such as diabetes or cystic fibrosis. Professor James Watson, one of the scientists who discovered DNA, recently argued for the extension of this approach if we ever discover a gene for homosexuality. What if scientists could manage to isolate the gene that accounts for our yearning for God? Eugenics is now poised to move to an altogether more sophisticated level, no longer mopping up nature's mistakes by abortion, but preventing their emergence by modifying and remaking human nature.

Today none of this is far fetched, one critical consideration is that the remaking of man has not emerged incidentally to the general direction taken by contemporary science, but now constitutes one of its major objectives. We are so used to this that many do not appreciate the novelty of the development. These are factors beyond the advance of science which are also at work to facilitate this reshaping. The absence of legislation, or government disinterest, together with the eclipse of God and diminished respect for any normative version of human nature all mean that for some, or many, scientists, the major constraint on human biological experimentation is the fear of catastrophic unforeseen consequences.

We all know of Nietzsche's infamous declaration that "God is dead." In making this claim Nietzsche is sometimes linked to Dostoyevsky, who in his major novels argued that if there is no God, "then everything is permitted." For both writers, but especially for Nietzsche, the more important dimension of this argument is not so much what it becomes possible to *do* in the wake of the death of God, as what it become possible to *think* and *desire*. In Nietzsche's view, Christian revelation, with its insistence on a higher and greater reality beyond the reality of human life constrains the possibilities of human existence, not least by constraining what it is possible to imagine ourselves doing. For example: attempting to fertilize human ova with the spermatozoa of a rat, or an orangutan, continues to be "unthinkable" in an important sense to faithful Christians – and to many other people. These are not ideas that would normally or spontaneously occur to us, and if and when they did occur, they are not ideas that we would entertain with anything other than horror. But when the sense of God has been eclipsed, this very gradually ceases to be the case. What was once morally repugnant becomes scientifically interesting. The horizon which revelation once placed around existence falls away, leaving man surrounded by "the roar of the boundless." This risk brings catastrophe and terrible human suffering. But for Nietzsche and those like him, the death of God means a new and exhilarating freedom – to think and do what it was not possible to think and do before.

This wrong and ultimately unsustainable notion of freedom continues to have powerful appeal for many moderns. We see it clearly in the notion common to many of our disenchanted young people that a rich and fulfilled life is one where the individuals has *experienced* as much as possible, irrespective of the nature of those experiences and the harm they may do physically, morally and spiritually. But it is among intellectuals and scientists in our society that Nietzsche's concept of freedom has also been most influential, even when Nietzsche's authorship is not recognized. The hostility of a significant group of intellectuals and scientists toward orthodox Christianity, perhaps particularly in the United States, flows in part from the steadfast way in which the Church has resisted this spurious notion of freedom and insisted that science and all scholarly endeavor must be subordinated to the service of authentically human values. But I also suspect that the roots of the animosity between the new class elites and the Church go even deeper than this.

Writing in 1971, when Communist oppression still flourished in Europe and the USSR, George Steiner remarked on "the brain-hammering strangeness of the monotheistic idea."[13] The concept of the Mosaic God is a unique fact in human history, without parallel in any time or place. It combines an injunction to almost impossible transcendence with a system of moral demands unequaled in history. On the one hand,

> brain and conscience are commanded to vest belief, obedience, love in an abstraction purer, more inaccessible to ordinary sense than is the highest of mathematics.[14]

In addition to this, there is the moral demand of monotheism. As Steiner says,

> Because the words are so familiar, yet too great for ready use, we tend to forget or merely conventionalize the extremity of their call. Only he who loses his life, in the fullest sense of sacrificial self-denial, shall find life. The kingdom is for the naked, for those who have willingly stripped themselves of every belonging, of every sheltering egoism. There is no salvation in the middle places.[15]

It is Steiner's controversial and daring contention that Western man, recognizing the supreme value of this idea,

---

[13] George Steiner, *In Bluebeard's Castle* (London, 1971), p. 36.
[14] *Ibid.*
[15] *Ibid.*, 39.

but filled with self-reproach from this inability to realize it, turned on the original bearers of the message of the Covenant – the Jews – in a way which ultimately culminated in the Holocaust.[16] "The summons to perfection" which monotheism "sought to impose on the current and currency of Western life" enforced "ideals [and] norms of conduct out of all natural grasp." Impossible to realize, they nevertheless weighed heavily on individual lives, building up in the subconscious deep loathings and murderous resentments. "The mechanism in simple but primordial:

> We have most those who hold out to us a goal, an ideal, a visionary promise which, even though we have stretched our muscles to the utmost, we cannot reach, which slips, again and again, just out of range of our racked fingers – yet, and this is crucial, which remains profoundly desirable, which we cannot reject because we fully acknowledge its supreme value.[17]

This provocative analysis might help explain the compulsive hostility among new class elites towards the orthodox monotheistic religions which refuse to compromise the hard teachings. I certainly believe it helps explain the systematic attempt of the communists to eradicate Christianity. In a different way it also enable us to identify some of the psychological sources of the opposition and personal hostility to the arguments for design in molecular biology explained so lucidly to us yesterday by Dr. Michael Behe. As did Hans Kornby a distinguished British biologist remarked at a seminar in Boston this week, "For scientists theology is like a lady of ill repute. No one want to be seen with her in public, but many use her by night or weekend." Even in the age of science, where the sense of God has been eclipsed for many Westerners, the claims of monotheistic revelation, continue to trouble and annoy those who would wish to be free of its demands, to escape successfully from

16 *Ibid.*, 38–42.
17 *Ibid.*, 41.

their guilt. Our task in this situation must be to keep the reality and central importance of the one true God in the public mind, in spite of the constant hostile pressure among the elites and the cheerful and careless agnosticism of others. Many of our own young Catholics will need to be given good reasons for believing in God's existence and shown His love in our practice. In doing all this, we must recognize that we cannot hope for easy approval. But if science and technology are to serve human life rather than dominate it, we have no choice. The mistaken individualistic notion of freedom so influential in our age must be opposed by authentic freedom lined to truth and producing real human service. Science and society will benefit from this in the long run, although the working out of these tensions over the generations will be a fascinating struggle, with the Brave New World of Aldous Huxley seeming a liklier immediate destination than the grim constraints of Orwell's 1984.

3. What is to be done?

A pamphlet of Lenin in 1902 was entitled *What is to be done?* This remains the crucial question, although mapping the territory and analyzing the situation are essential prerequisites for action, and I still wish to say a few words about the crucial group in this discussion re Generation X, those born between 1963 and 1980 and their children. They take for granted the fact that they live in a scientific-technological world, and find it difficult to imagine living without the advantages of such a world (John Vernon's son). They would be dimly aware that 95% of all scientists in human history are now living (still a small minority of the generation), but little vexed by the origins of the universe, the neurochemistry of consciousness, genetic planning of the species or the nature of matter, much less by any moral or theological problems attendant on such scientific work. In fact most have never been involved in a church, or even a Sunday school (this is certainly true in Australia; perhaps less true in the United States); they have watched 5000 hours of television by the age of five. Many have suffered from the divorce of their parents and are reluctant to make life-long commitments, while inclined to delay child-bearing. Feminism is no longer a burning issue, because male and female equality is taken for granted and it is assumed that women should be church ministers. At least in Australia, motherhood has replaced homosexuality as a topic that should not be discussed. The educated among Generation X are also seriously tempted by post-modernism; inclined like us, to the easier short-term solutions, to relativism, to avoiding the examination of grand themes on the meaning of life. Some of course insist there are no such truths.

The overwhelming majority of Generation X still identify themselves as Christians; a bigger majority are monotheists. In times of public crises many turn to the Christian churches. Interestingly enough, the irreligious minority does not like to be described as neo-pagan (which it certainly is), probably because it senses that majority opinion is opposed to paganism.

A preliminary conclusion is that it will take much wise and persevering effort and more than a touch of luck and grace to enlist majority support among Generation X and X + 1 to oppose the Culture of Death on abortion and euthanasia, although the struggle to defend heterosexual marriage should be less difficult. In the democracies, religious leadership to inform public opinion and legislative struggle and political activity will be needed to constrain the more grotesque forms of experimentation touching humans, (with some hope of success) and we should be able to achieve continuing majority belief in the One True God, providing we realize that this, and more particularly the Divinity of Christ within the Catholic community will be severely contested.

A couple of small personal reminiscences will help explain my approach in listing my recommendations.

My work as a priest and then a bishop has meant that I have traveled a lot by air, both within Australia and internationally. I always travel in uniform, dressed as a priest, because it pays to advertise. During long flights most in the next seat do not want to talk much, but there are some exceptions. One was an Australian businessman who seemed prosperous, was certainly confident and wanted to talk, indeed philosophize. He had some land he thought the Church might be interested to buy, etc., etc. He then explained that the secret of success in life and in business was to identify what are the few key issues, and find the right answers to these few. If these right solutions are found, generally the multifarious secondary problems fall into place.

My second reminiscence draws on many years as a junior school football coach, which I thoroughly enjoyed. Experience taught me that when the game started to flow against my young team, many players became rattled, did strange things like attempting the impossible, playing to the strengths of the opposition, or abandoning the most basic procedures. The only way to play against strong opposition was to remember and follow our basic ground rules. When those were in place, then we could afford to be more adventurous: we did not always win, but we generally used our strengths to best advantage.

Church people can often be more like my young football players than my business acquaintance. They can forget the fundamental point that our success and failure can only be judged in Christ Our Lord's terms.

My first recommendation is about ways and means; to encourage every variety of Catholic teacher to use all available technology and so do two things: reach out beyond the Catholic community, as well as instructing committed and cultural Catholics. It has been remarked that the Protestant Reformation would have been impossible without the invention of printing. Luther was a masterly publicist. It was the Lutherans who first invented catechisms, while the Catholics were hampered by their use of Latin, and by poor and infrequent popular teaching. We were behind the play then technologically, but risk having learnt that lesson to well by too much reliance, now on printed media (books and Catholic newspapers) and speaking only to the Catholic community, in an age of radio, television, videos and the Internet, and many interested, uncommitted outsiders.

In the Western world there will continue to be an exodus from faith, or at least from regular practice. But if we face outwards in our parishes and agencies through service, and use technology and the secular media to explain our morals and our faith (something the Holy Father does so outstandingly), there should be a balancing stream of converts and returnees, many of them damaged by contemporary society and others, while very successful in the eyes of the world, still personally empty and dissatisfied.

The regular practice of religion now parallels the patterns of employment across the generations since the Industrial Revolution. Once generations of men in the one family had the same type of job. With the rise of prosperity, migration and social mobility, many sons held job different from their fathers, but often for a lifetime. Now many women and men have a variety of jobs in one lifetime, and too many have no job or long periods of unemployment. Being a committed Catholic will be more like this, with many committed parents seeing their children drift from practice, and individuals themselves, shifting position across their lifetime; all of this because of the steady flow of news and views hostile to Christian belief and practice, and because of the weakened sense of tradition in the West. This is another reason to reach beyond the churchgoers.

As a digression, I am inclined to think that in this age of fast, scientifically induced change, we should make an explicit and regular appeal, counter-culture as it is, to tradition, the "the democracy of the deed" pointing out the advantages of knowing where we come from and of knowing the wisdom that has sustained men and women for millennia. I believe there is a religious market for tradition especially among the young!

Whatever of tradition, when I preach each Sunday in my

cathedral I reach some hundreds of believers, who need encouragement and information. With articles or interviews of a few paragraphs in a secular newspaper, or even some minutes on television or the radio, we reach tens or hundreds of thousands. Recently an elderly priest writer in Sydney launched his own website on the Internet, accompanied by good press in our national newspaper. He claimed 32,000 hits in the first 36 hours, and 50,000 hits by the end of the first week![18]

Second level consequences also follow from the involvement of Catholic teachers public debate and discussion on issues important to us or society. Churchgoers are generally heartened by these signs of life and Catholic youngsters are reminded of our claims, of where they should belong.

Such activity also focuses attention on where the basic tension should be, i.e., between the Church and world, and not between Catholics. Public differences among Catholics are sometimes necessary in these times of division; but they are always unfortunate, never more than a second best.

Last year a coalition of all the Christian leaders in my state of Victoria objected to the exhibition in our government-financed state art gallery of a blasphemous photo of a crucifix in urine. As Catholic archbishop I also ledged a legal objection in our Supreme Court. Predictably we lost in law case, but unexpectedly the entire show, consisting almost entirely of pornography and blasphemy, was closed down and withdrawn.

The moral of the story for present purposes is that I received overwhelming Catholic support, public prayers for our campaign in a Jewish synagogue, and letters of endorsement from the Moslem community and from some religious congregations not usually listed among my public admirers.

More idiosyncratically my second recommendation in this age of science is to insist that future priests are thoroughly formed, not just in sound Catholic doctrine, but

---

[18] Website address is www.costello.au.com.

more importantly in the practice of pray and an understanding and love of Christian spirituality. We need God-
centered priests.

In this Vatican Two age of the laity such a high priority
for priests might be politically incorrect even hazardous.
But Our Lord himself was quite explicit about the need for
fishers of men, for shepherds and for workers in the harvest
(although this final reference is capable of wider meanings).

As the pressures against full Catholic living continue
from outside and within the Catholic community, we shall
continue to need a network of local leaders who know that
the central external challenge is against God; who cannot
be knocked off balance into believing the threats are elsewhere, much less inveigled into believing the answers to
our problems will be found by "improving"/softening up
Christ's teachings.

Regular prayer is necessary for this steadiness as well as
a clear head, accurate knowledge of the tradition and personal and intellectual self-confidence. To achieve this every
priest needs a sound formation in philosophy, with
Thomism as a significant constituent, and a goodly number
of years in an updated version of the Tridentine seminary,
which was the greatest gift to the Church from that long,
difficult but profoundly important Council that promised
the Counter-Reformation.

Whatever the gains and losses might be in the future in
the Catholic universities and universities more generally;
whatever the consequences of the convulsive changes in
religious life, decline, disappearance and vigorous new life
(often in canonically hybrid communities), the parish network has to survive. And its leaders have to be prepared for
the bleakest winter as well as for the springtime.

Many other things might be said, particularly on the difficulties of a community who finds its truth in a two thousand year old apostolic tradition; whose Redeemer and
founder lived at the beginning of our era. All this in an age
geared to the future, to progress and innovation.

But enough is enough.

A final word about the importance of maintaining Catholic self-confidence, a worthy sense of identity, as the human framework for the flame of faith, for personal conversion.

4. Conclusion.

We should not be daunted by our situation, remembering the Christ we follow and the saints, martyrs and writers of two millennia who fire our imagination. As G. K. Chesterton reminded us, "It was no flock of sheep the Christian shepherd was leading, but a herd of bulls and tigers, of terrible ideals and devouring doctrines.[19] May the good God preserve an increasing number of us from the tyranny of personal consciences shaped by metaphysical muddle, fear of public opinion and an all too easy hedonism. May the same good God preserve more and more of us from the pathetic illusions that religious vitality can be repurchased without duty, discipline and explicit faith; that our guilts can be banished without repentance and God's forgiveness.

The only way forward is to embrace the love, the steel and the romance of orthodoxy. With the grace of God, prayer, learning and hard work, it is not beyond our capacity to have "the equilibrium of a man behind wildly rushing horses, seeming to stoop this way and to sway that way, yet in every attitude having the grace of statuary and the accuracy of arithmetic."[20] We must never forget orthodox church was never respectable, never took the tame course. Let me conclude with that famous and inspiring passage from Chesterton's "Orthodoxy."

> To have fallen into any of those open traps of error
> and exaggeration which fashion after fashion and sect

[19] G.K. Chesterton, *Orthodoxy* (New York, 1990 [1908]), p. 100.

[20] *Ibid.*, pp. 100–101.

after sect set along the historic path of Christendom –
that would indeed have been simple. It is always simple to fall; there are an infinity of angels at which one
falls – only one – at which one stands. To have fallen
into any one of the fads from Gnosticism to Christian
Science would indeed have been obvious and tame.
But to have avoided them all; has been one whirling
adventure; and in my vision the heavenly chariot flies
thundering through the ages, the dull heresies sprawl-
ing and prostrate, the wild truth reeling but erect,[21]

even and especially in an age of science.

[21] *Ibid.*, p. 101.

FELLOWSHIP OF CATHOLIC SCHOLARS

Membership Information
http://www4.allencol.edu/~philtheo/FCS/

Statement of Purpose

(1) We Catholic scholars in various disciplines join in fellowship in order to serve Jesus Christ better by helping one another in our work and by putting our abilities more fully at the service of the Catholic faith.

(2) We wish to form a fellowship of scholars who see their intellectual work as expressing the service they owe to God. To Him we give thanks for our Catholic faith and for every opportunity He gives us to serve that faith.

(3) We wish to form a fellowship of Catholic scholars open to the work of the Holy Spirit within the Church. Thus we wholeheartedly accept and support the renewal of the Church of Christ undertaken by Pope John XXIII, shaped by Vatican II, and carried on by succeeding pontiffs.

(4) We accept as the rule of our life and thought the entire faith of the Catholic Church. This we see not merely in solemn definitions but in the ordinary teaching of the Pope and those bishops in union with him, and also embodied in those modes of worship and ways of Christian life, of the present as of the past, which have been in harmony with the teaching of St. Peter's successors in the See of Rome.

(6) To contribute to this sacred work, our fellowship will strive to:

> * Come to know and welcome all who share our purpose;
> * Make known to one another our various competencies and interests;

* Share our abilities with one another unstintingly in our efforts directed to our common purpose;

* Cooperate in clarifying the challenges which must be met;

* Help one another to evaluate critically the variety of responses which are proposed to these challenges;

* Communicate our suggestions and evaluations to members of the Church who might find them helpful;

* Respond to requests to help the Church in its task of guarding the faith as inviolable and defending it with fidelity;

* Help one another to work through, in scholarly and prayerful fashion and without public dissent, any problem which may arise from magisterial teaching.

(7) With the grace of God for which we pray, we hope to assist the whole Church to understand its own identity more clearly, to proclaim the joyous Gospel of Jesus more confidently, and to carry out its redemptive mission of all humankind more effectively.

To apply for membership, contact:

Rev. Thomas F. Dailey, O.S.F.S.
FCS Executive Secretary
Allentown College of St. Francis de Sales
2755 Station Avenue
Center Valley, PA 18034–9568
Tel.: (610) 282–1100, Ext. 1464
E-mail: tfdO@email.allencol.edu

Member Benefits

FCS Quarterly – All members receive four issues annually. The 50-page publication includes:

* President's page
* Scholarly articles

* Documentation
* Bulletin Board (news)
* Book Reviews

Membership Directory – All members receive the annually updated listing of FCS members in the U.S.A. and abroad.

National Conventions – All members are invited to participate in the annual gathering. The typical program includes:
* Daily Mass
* Six scholarly Sessions
* Keynote Address
* Banquet and Awards

Regular members receive a copy of the *Proceedings* of each convention.

National Awards – The Fellowship grants the following awards, usually presented during its annual convention:

> * The *Cardinal Wright Award* is given *annually* to a Catholic adjudged to have done an outstanding service for the Church in the tradition of the late Cardinal John J. Wright, Bishop of Pittsburgh and later Prefect, Congregation for the Clergy. Previous recipients are:
>
> 1979 – Rev. Msgr. George A. Kelly
> 1980 – Dr. William E. May
> 1981 – Dr. James Hitchcock
> 1982 – Dr. Germain Grisez
> 1983 – Rev. John Connery, S.J.
> 1984 – Rev. John Hardon, S.J.
> 1985 – Dr. Herbert Ratner
> 1986 – Dr. Joseph P. Scottino
> 1987 – Rev. Joseph Farraher, S.J. & Rev. Joseph Fessio, S.J.
> 1988 – Rev. John Harvey, O.S.F.S.

1989 – Dr. John Finnis
1990 – Rev. Ronald Lawler, O.F.M. Cap
1991 – Rev. Francis Caravan, S.J.
1992 – Rev. Donald J. Keefe, S.J.
1993 – Dr. Janet E. Smith
1994 – Dr. Jude P. Dougherty
1995 – Rev. Msgr. William B. Smith
1996 – Dr. Ralph McInerny
1997 – Rev. James V. Schall, S.J.
1998 – Mr. Kenneth D. Whitehead & Rev.
          Msgr. Michael Wrenn
1999 – Dr. Robert P. George

* The *Cardinal O'Boyle Award* is given *occasionally* to an individual whose actions demonstrate a courage and witness for the Catholic Church similar to that exhibited by the late Cardinal Patrick A. O'Boyle, Archbishop of Washington, in light of dissenting pressures in our society.

1988 – Rev. John C. Ford, S.J.
1991 – Mother Angelica, P.C.P.A., EWTN
1995 – John and Sheila Kippley, Couple to
          Couple League
1997 – Rep. Henry J. Hyde, (R-IL)